PIÑA COLADAS
AND THE PEARLY GATES

THE POWDER ROOM BOOK SERIES

Reflections from the Powder Room on The Love Dare

Reflections on The Shack

Reflections on 90 Minutes in Heaven

Piña Coladas and the Pearly Gates

AVAILABLE FROM DESTINY IMAGE PUBLISHERS

Piña Coladas
and the Pearly Gates

A Powder Room Book

Book 4

Writers: Shae Cooke, Tammy Fitzgerald, Donna Scuderi, Angela Rickabaugh Shears

Page Layout: Dominique Abney

Ambient Press

P.O. Box 310, Shippensburg, PA 17257-0310

For a U.S. bookstore nearest you, call 1-800-722-6774.

For more information on foreign distributors, call 717-532-3040.

Reach us on the Internet: www.ambientpress.com.

Trade Paper ISBN 13: 978-0-7684-3197-1

Hard Cover ISBN 13: 978-0-7684-3412-5

Large Print ISBN 13: 978-0-7684-3413-2

Ebook ISBN 13: 978-0-7684-9067-1

For Worldwide Distribution, Printed in the U.S.A.

1 2 3 4 5 6 7 8 9 10 11 / 13 12 11 10

CONTENTS

PREFACE

Ala Shae

Prior to becoming a Christian, and even while spiritually young, I occasionally had "one too many," sometimes to the point of *tipsiness* (divas don't get "drunk"!). As I matured (and God dealt with some major flaws), and as I learned how to hear God's voice, it seemed He was asking me, "Why do you want to drink?" Indeed, what was my motive? I tempered my drinking somewhat to the occasional glass of wine as I sought to investigate the reasons why I drank, and examined my heart. It's not that God convicted me that drinking was a sin, mind you.

Today, before I even take a sip, I ask myself, "Why do I want a drink right now?" And in my spirit ask, "God, is this OK with You, or would You rather I not?" Listen, I want to be ready for *any* assignment God gives me or for a potential divine visitation, so if He says, "Honey, hold off the sap for today," I will hold off with joy and expectation!

Now that I have drinking under control, I am in the process of examining my affinity for anything with sole! I would sooner buy a pair of espadrilles to cheer me up than down a good vintage Mouton Cadet, so it appears God isn't finished with me yet. Perhaps when next we meet in the Powder Room, we can touch on the subject of shoeaholicism. Papa? Anyone? 52 pairs and counting…up! Puhleeeasseee help!

INTRODUCTION

Not to Condone or Condemn

Hmmm…to drink or not to drink, that's the question for many people—especially Christians. From some churches using wine during Communion to others strictly prohibiting any use, from Christians brewing beer at home to those advocating complete abstinence, this controversial subject touches cultures and consciences worldwide.

These reflections from the Powder Room not only uncork myths and mire, but also add bubbly banter and intoxicating intrigue to decades' worth of dilemmas.

Yes Jesus drank wine, but was it "purified water," as some contend? Yes the Bible says not to be drunkards, but does that include a beer while watching a football game? Yes some people become alcoholics, but not everyone.

Someone quipped that this book should have been titled *WWJD—What Would Jesus Drink*. Well, that's what we explore, as well as what has been and is being said about Christians drinking alcohol. We thoroughly consider—in a Thoroughly-Modern-Millie kind of way—all aspects of this Christian dilemma, including current, historical, biblical, medical, spiritual, emotional, physical, and even criminal issues.

We write not to condone or condemn—but to bring a variety of views to the table and serve up fare full of robust flavors and fizz.

CHAPTER 1

Don't Ask, Don't Tell

Angela

We sit beside a dear friend every week (well, almost) in church who occasionally enjoys a "nice glass of wine" with her husband. Another close friend wouldn't even consider having lunch in a restaurant that has a bar section. Extended Christian family members expected an "open bar" at our youngest daughter's wedding reception. While a neighbor showed me a recent photo of herself and one of her daughters—apologizing for the beer the daughter is holding.

In response to an e-mail sent to Christian friends, family,

and clients about the topic of drinking alcohol, I received varied and soul-stirring answers. Because of the surprisingly overwhelming number of responses, a sampling of responses follow, and others are scattered throughout:

- I do drink, and yet have come to drink less and less because it destroys the house (my little round body!) that God gave me to use while I'm here on this earth. I work so hard on exercising in the morning that I hate to mess up all the good that I've done in the evening with a drink or two!

- Drinking? What's wrong with drinking?

- I have two views. (1) For me, as someone who comes from a family full of substance abusers, I steer clear of alcohol. As a Christian, I stay away from alcohol because it is such an abused substance in our society. We live in context. If the color green in our society signified infidelity, I wouldn't wear green. It just happens to be my favorite color, but since I represent the King of kings, I would keep green in my heart and wait until Heaven to wear it. (2) Also as a Christian, I don't feel that I can condone or condemn another Christian who drinks alcohol. If they drink abusively, that is plainly an issue of sin and should be addressed as such. Actually I shared three views, but I never could count. :-)

- EVERYTHING IN MODERATION. Drink

to hydrate, drink to toast, but don't drink to unconsciousness.

- There was a professional snake handler who had a pet rattlesnake. He was sure the snake would never bite him. After all, he knew how to "handle" it. One day the rattlesnake did what rattlesnakes do—it bit the man; a day later the man died. Drinking alcohol is like playing with a rattlesnake, you may think you can handle it but it will eventually surprise and bite you. I experienced the pain of its bite for 23 years of my life, but I slew my rattlesnake when I met Jesus, and my lips have not touched alcohol for the past 19 years. —Dr. Keith Johnson, The-ConfidenceCoach.com

- I don't drink, I don't chew, and I don't keep company with those who do.

Donna

Ah…the "alcohol rub," to frame a pun poorly. My friends, like yours, Angela, have wide-ranging views. I surmise them mostly through the ether—Facebook posts, vacation snapshots, that sort of thing. Apart from these divulgences, the Christian "policy" regarding alcohol seems to be: "Don't ask; don't tell."

The invisible fence is partly cultural. For some, wine is as essential to the dining experience as a fine cut of meat. Cultural differences also cloud the original meaning of Scriptures written in the context of antiquity (another topic that's sure to come up soon).

Yet, I believe the silence has more to do with respect and comfort zones. Most Christians don't want to render condemnation or division by splitting doctrinal hairs. But we're also squeamish about getting into other people's "space." A word or two about alcohol from the pulpit is OK, but in conversation? Not so much.

But, bravo to several friends who shared their opinions (all I had to do was ask). Here are a few:

- I was raised in a "dry" home. We didn't think Christians should drink; so we didn't. What I have come to accept is that just because I don't drink doesn't mean it's terrible for other responsible Christians to do so—as long as they are well aware of what their limitations are— which is another gray area.

- The Bible sanctions the drinking of alcohol. The problem is becoming drunk and no longer in full control of your faculties. The Bible says that you should not be drunk in the flesh, but drunk in the Spirit. I also feel it's important not to be a stumbling block to others. Just because you don't have a problem with alcohol doesn't mean it's OK to drink and cause someone who has an issue to stumble.

- I love God and am displeased when He is displeased with me. I also love an occasional ice cold beer, Margarita, or glass of red wine.

Scripture does not necessarily forbid Christians from drinking these beverages. Ecclesiastes 9:7, Psalms 104:14-15, and Amos 9:14 prove that. The epistles, which I believe are instructions to the Church, make it clear that drunkenness and addiction are sin and that our bodies are not to be mastered by anything (see 1 Cor. 6:12; Eph. 5:18). The issue is self-control.

- I believe we live under the law of the Spirit of life in Christ Jesus and not under the Old Covenant. Moderation, self-control, and not grieving the Spirit are our keys to conduct.

- As long as you drink in moderation and are not causing harm to others or yourself, I don't think alcohol is bad, [provided you are] aware of your own body and aware of those around you.

- As Christians, we should want to keep ourselves as pure as can be. We will never be perfect; however, we are to be the salt of the earth and the light of the world. People are always watching us. We need to do whatever it takes to separate ourselves from the world and be "peculiar" (see 1 Pet. 2:9 KJV).

Tammy

Alcohol—what a topic! Especially as a young twenty-something worshiping in the church and working in the world, it can be a little crazy adapting to the different views around me between church on Sunday and work on Monday. It's like hopping back and forth between a jacuzzi and the North Atlantic in January—the temperature of the water can change that suddenly!

Outside of Christian circles, alcohol barely registers as any different from the rest of the beverage menu. (The number one distinction is probably price, yowzers!) But within the Church… well, opinions are certainly varied, but it seems like everyone is at least drawing a line *somewhere*, as opposed to drawing no lines at all.

I attended a private Christian college that had its own little Prohibition Era in full swing for anyone and everyone connected to the university. After that, I attended a state school where orientation included what streets to stay away from on Friday night—unless you were there to party. After that, I worked in a school where the number one faculty hangout on weekends was a local bar. A day or two later in class, I might hear a sermon on the evils of addiction, alcohol featuring heavily in that message.

To make a long story short, I've got my hands full figuring out where I stand. And my peers are in the same boat. I asked a few of them what they thought:

- Drinking in excess is the problem. Too much of anything is not good; that also goes for food, sex, money, and so on. And drinking for the sole purpose of getting drunk is just stupid.

- The Bible doesn't say not to drink alcohol, it says not to *be* drunk. So, alcohol in moderation is OK. Though if you want to be technical about it, the Bible says "be not drunk *with wine,*" so getting drunk with beer is OK. (He's totally kidding, by the way.) LOL. ^_~

- I personally think that it seems to be very easy to get drunk when out drinking with friends, due to the whole peer-pressure thing, plus losing track of how much you drank while chatting and such. So I only drink when in small groups, say, a glass of wine when out on a dinner date with my husband, or a small party at a family member's house.

- Alcohol is so evil. I don't want to be anywhere near it.

- I feel like I hear more clearly from the Spirit of the Lord when I've had a little wine.

Wow. I'll be honest, I personally find some of this to be off the deep end. I've got one thing clear though—when it comes to forming a position on alcohol, you can pick your poison, for sure! Hmm…I wonder if there are more opinions on drinking than there are vintages of wine out there today?

Shae

———— ⌘ ————

Do blonde, middle-age opinions count, Tamster? *grin* My Christian friends, peers, family members, and colleagues comprise people from every age, occupation, background, caste, culture, and level of spiritual maturity imaginable: blue-collar workers and executives, students and homemakers, actors and producers, athletes and people with disabilities, pastors and international Christian leaders, editors and writers, oh, and executive shoppers—LOL. Of those, some have spiritual rags to riches stories and others were born and raised in spiritual affluence. Some drink and others do not. I have shared glasses of wine with some amazing Christians and I have abstained with equally incredible people. A pattern I do see emerging from the viewpoints already shared, and of what I know concerning my contacts, is that those who do imbibe obviously feel at some level that it is OK, but most interject caveats. Teetotalers—the ones who abstain because they feel that drinking is wrong, period, oppose with levels of greater fervency, and less leeway.

IMHO, it really is not about being bound to a "thou shalt not drink law" (if one exists), Old Covenant Law, self-induced law, or fabricated law, but about being bound to a *Living Person*, Christ Jesus. Nothing turns a not-yet-Christian or babe in Christ, (or young person, Tammy!) off more than sets of laws and countless rules do. Keeping such standards does not help anyone grow to any level of spiritual maturity. Adhering to rules did not help me in my early walk with God. Binding myself to, seeking and engaging in a true relationship experience with Christ gave me faith and enablement to discern and want right in my life. Filling myself with Him displaces sin and the potential to sin—for instance, over-indulging in a stellar Cabernet— and daily empowers me toward obedience and His will.

This is the beauty of Christianity, the heart of Christianity. The least can know Him in the deepest way imaginable without a smattering of theological understanding of precepts, the simplest without being bound to rules or condemned, such that a broken and rebellious teen turned wife turned divorcée turned blonde, single mother from the boonies of Canada can become an international writing evangelist, if God wills it. The more of Him I see, the less of everything else I need, and that includes the highs of chocolate, shoes, and the odd glass or two of wine! Judging from the fullness of my snack vault, wine cellar, closets, and growing midline, I need more time in that wonderful Secret Place of His Presence.

We need to take this matter up One-on-one with God, don't you think? My prayer is that as we uncork the issue, people of both convictions genuinely push aside religiosity or maverick thought and press into the Father's heart on the matter. To that end, I invite Him to break through our wonderings, wanderings, and beliefs on this controversial subject, and give us true revelation of what He desires of us.

Your Reflections

_____

_____

_____

_____

_____

_____

_____

_____

_____

_____

_____

_____

_____

Your Reflections

_____

_____

_____

_____

_____

_____

_____

_____

_____

_____

_____

_____

_____

_____

_____

_____

_____

_____

_____

_____

_____

_____

_____

_____

_____

_____

_____

_____

_____

_____

_____

_____

_____

_____

_____

_____

_____

_____

_____

_____

_____

_____

_____

_____

_____

_____

_____

_____

_____

_____

_____

_____

_____

_____

_____

_____

_____

_____

_____

_____

_____

_____

CHAPTER 2

Damned if You Do—Prude if You Don't?

Donna

Choosing between being "damned" or a "prude" leaves me wanting. Besides, I'm pretty sure you can end up being neither—or both.

Until my mid-teens, I was a Roman Catholic. Apart from knowing that drunkenness was not an aspiration encouraged by my mentor, Sister Mary Lambert, I don't remember knowing what the Catholic position on alcohol was. I've since asked my friend Google for help. Here's what my cyber-sleuthing revealed: "The official Roman Catholic view is that total abstinence (except for religious communion) is desirable and virtuous…. On the other hand, drinking in moderation is approved"[1]

So abstinence is not prudish and drinking in moderation is not damning. Pope John Paul II adds a practical touch: "Love is the point of departure and the final goal of the family…. The example which parents offer to their children in showing that love, which implies mutual respect, forgiveness and moderation in their own behaviour, will mark the path for their children to follow."[2] My parents' example would have pleased the Holy Father.

My first non-RCC church was charismatic and nondenominational. The pastor's views on alcohol were black and white: He advocated abstinence, and everyone knew exactly where he stood. It made for awkward moments at weddings as "the damned" sheep nervously imbibed under the pastor's watchful eye. "Uhhh…Pastor…have you tried this gluten-free, non-alcoholic wine yet? It's amaaaazing!"

My third church was affiliated with the Assemblies of God, whose position paper on alcohol states: "…We urge all believers to avoid the satanic tool of alcohol which destroys lives, damns souls, and blights society…."[3] (That's almost "damning," but not quite.) "The call to holy living and to total abstinence is most appropriate for [those expecting] the soon return of Jesus…. As we watch and pray for the return of Jesus, our senses should be as sharp and clear as they can possibly be."[4] I'm still not getting the "prudish" vibe; this guidance is 100-proof, however.

My fourth church is also nondenominational and charismatic, but my current pastor's view is slightly different: "Drinking alcohol is a great dilemma within the Church…. Is it OK? How much is OK? Only wine? But it all has alcohol, right? If I say it's OK, then I'll have to say how much is OK…right? The Bible provides ample examples of drinking to celebrate. It provides examples of drinking to the point of drunkenness resulting in bad things happening. We can look to our own families' lives…. Overuse, abuse, and reliance upon [alcohol] ultimately brings destruction…. So, go ahead with a big, yellow caution sign."

No labels. Just know thyself and thy drink's pitfalls.

Tammy

A few years ago, as I mentioned, I graduated from a completely "dry" university. (Now, granted, it wasn't a church, but after chapel five days a week for four years? Yeah, I'd say it was pretty close, LOL.) Their policy went so far as to forbid all students—whether under 21 or over—from not only drinking, but even from being in a place where alcohol was served. Reading through their official policy again (it hasn't changed at all since I was a student) it's interesting to note that the school makes virtually no distinction between the *use* and *abuse* of alcohol, even for those of legal age.

For a while there, I was under the impression that most Christians reviled alcohol as sinful. I spent my earliest years as a

Christian in churches that were very clear on their "dry" position, much like my university. Honestly, it was a little tough—opposing moderate drinking for legal adults had never occurred to me before my salvation. I couldn't see why it was suddenly an issue, but I was a young believer and accepted what I was taught.

When it got to the point where I couldn't be around alcohol drinkers anymore without feeling awkward, I began to realize that I'd developed a wrong attitude. I had become judgmental, and it was hurting my witness. It was hard for me to demonstrate openness and Christ-like love because I was too busy being shocked by the presence of a *beverage!*

I'm so glad the Lord led me to different churches after that. I've grown so much more in churches that don't have a "hard and fast" abstinence approach, because I'm confronted instead with the challenging task of learning to make my own decisions and responsibly handle Christian liberty. That takes maturity! To me, it was a matter of where I was getting my final guidance—the church that said "no alcohol," or the Spirit of the Lord? When I had a firm and final human voice directing my choice, I didn't need to ask the Spirit what He thought. Yikes!

Since graduating college, I would guess that most of my experience in the church has been under official policies like the last one you quoted, Donna. While I do still know of churches that condemn all alcohol consumption as sinful, it seems like most take a more moderate position. But hey, I'm a fan of anything that helps young Christians grow into spiritual maturity! As long as we're growing up strong in our love relationship with Him, I've got no beef with anyone! ^_^

Angela

Hmmm…I think I'll wear my prude pink with pride—after all, I'm carrying on a family tradition. When going through my father's things after he passed away in 1984 (my mother had passed away seven years earlier), I found an old, tattered and faded 3x6 card with a pen and ink drawing of Dr. N.W. Tracy (still not sure who he was) and the words, "I DARE TO DO RIGHT! With Malice toward none and Charity for all. I, the undersigned, pledge my word and honor, GOD HELPING ME, to abstain from all intoxicating liquors, as a beverage, and that I will by all honorable means, encourage others to abstain." The card was signed by my paternal grandparents, who were born in the early 1870s.

I attend church services in the same beautiful brick building with stained-glass windows whose congregation was established in 1764—the same place where my parents and grandparents worshiped. But I doubt the couple who pledged their "word and honor" would appreciate the current stance about "intoxicating liquors" of the Presbyterian Church. From the PCUSA Web site:

> The former United Presbyterian Church in North America was a temperance church—advocating total abstinence—right up until its absorption in the new UPCUSA in 1957. The 1961 statement…The Church and the Problem of Alcohol provided the first comprehensive statement on the subject to recognize the fact that many Presbyterians do drink and suggests

that the problems of alcohol could be resolved by the responsible drinking for those who choose to drink and abstinence for others.

In 1986, the "reunited church" issued the following "general principles" that "should guide personal and corporate choices: Abstention in all situations should be supported and encouraged. Moderate drinking in low-risk situations should not be opposed. Heavy drinking in any situation should be vigorously discouraged. Any drinking in high-risk situations (e.g., during pregnancy or before driving an automobile) should be vigorously discouraged, as should all illegal drinking."

The current pastor of "our family" church responded: "My quick answer is that Scripture would seem to indicate that while drunkenness is forbidden, the drinking of wine, even by Jesus himself, was allowed. Jesus even turned water into wine. Like many other issues, we are to use our freedom in Christ responsibly."

Friend and pastor of South Mountain Chapel Brethren in Christ David A. Erisman says:

> [My] personal stand on alcohol, and other potentially harmful items (except Mt. Dew!), is that my body is the temple of the Lord and I really want to try my best to honor Him with what I place into His temple. This includes alcohol, drugs, nicotine, overeating, etc. Does this mean I think Believers who drink are not going to make it into Heaven—absolutely not! They simply have not been convicted by the Lord the same way I have been on this topic. I can't stand the taste

of alcohol! I'm a pastor in the Brethren in Christ denomination—a small evangelical, peace-loving group of Believers. Our denomination's stance is similar to mine; except they allow for consuming alcohol in moderation. I think it boils down to life habits/choices that we make because of our convictions.

Shae

"God helping me..." as your grandparents' pledge card beautifully put it, Angela, is the point. Ouch Chihuahua. Until I could lay aside the belief that God was a far off and gavel-toting, long-bearded, eyebrow-furrowed deity who viewed me as a bull's-eye for His full quiver of lightning bolts, to the thunderous applause of the cheering heavenly host when He hit the mark; and believe in a loving Father with my best interest at heart, fear, not of the reverent kind, coerced at least a measure of acquiescent obedience from me. The hell-fire and brimstone rule approach of many churches may work for some people, but it caused a rebellious spirit to arise in me, and I ran away from God in the spirit of Jonah, and figuratively rotted in the belly of the world for several years as a result. Thankfully, Love found me. It is so much better swaying to the will of the Father, being in love with the Father!

I am uncertain when or why the Christian church started to split off into different streams and denominations after Pentecost, but I think the flesh and fear got the better of us. Hence, the fabrication of divisive precepts, and perhaps the "thou shalt not booze it up" rule. Understandable, though, in light of ancient Judaic practices whereby the rabbis of the first century sought to protect The Law and built hedges of additional manmade laws around it as extra padding to ensure people did not break it. The thought was that if people could keep those devised laws, they would not come close to violating what God prohibited. For instance, to prevent accidentally taking God's name (*Yahweh*) in vain, they called Him *Adonai* meaning "Lord," or *Ha-shem* meaning "the Name." In an effort to prevent Exodus 23:19 from happening even a smidgen, that of not boiling a young goat in its mother's milk, (ee-ewe) the rabbis devised a law whereby a meal could not even be consumed in the presence of milk and meat together! Rah rah! Or should I say, "Baa-baa!"

In the same way, I surmise different denominations of the Church have initiated drinking laws, as well as others as well-intentioned padding for us, perchance as aids in winning the battle of the flesh, the law at war with the law of the mind, which brings us *"into captivity to the law of sin"* and death (see Rom. 7:23). The "don't drink the stuff at all" POV might be to prevent the worst from happening—the weakening of resolve not to sin. And, or, the opening of doors to all sorts of sins of the flesh, which are hard enough to resist in the manner of whatsoever a man sows he shall also reap…sow to the flesh, of the flesh reap corruption (see Gal. 6:7).

There is a struggle of the flesh, as transparent Paul confessed he had (see Rom. 7:18-20). Nevertheless, we really do need revelation of the New Law of the Spirit of life in Christ Jesus that frees us from the law of sin and death, damnation and prudeness ala Romans 8:2. When I count on His indwelling life to work through me I am able to exercise self-control in drinking and in those things my flesh would otherwise love to indulge! My hedge, therefore, is the Precious Person of the Holy Spirit. As a result, I have plenty of leftovers. Starbucks, Prada, Häagen-Dazs, vintage Penfolds Grange anyone?

Endnotes

1. David J. Hanson, *Preventing Alcohol Abuse* (Westport, CT: Praeger Publishers, 1995), 36, http://books.google.com/books?id=AWk8FGoJwWAC&printsec=copyright&source=gbs_pub_info_s&cad=2.

2. Pope John Paul II, "Address of Pope John Paul II to the Participants in the Thirty-first International Institute for the Prevention and Treatment of Alcoholism," (address, June 7, 1985), http://www.vatican.va/holy_father/john_paul_ii/speeches/1985/june/documents/hf_jp-ii_spe_19850607_convegno-alcoolismo_en.html.

3. General Council of the Assemblies of God, "Abstinence," (official statement approved by the General Presbytery of the Assemblies of God, August 6, 1985), 1, http://www.ag.org/top/Beliefs/Position_Papers/pp_downloads/pp_4187_abstinence.pdf.

4. Ibid., 4.

Your Reflections

_____

_____

_____

_____

_____

_____

_____

_____

_____

_____

_____

_____

_____

_____

_____

_____

_____

_____

_____

_____

_____

_____

_____

_____

_____

_____

_____

_____

_____

_____

_____

_____

_____

_____

_____

_____

_____

_____

_____

_____

_____

_____

_____

_____

_____

_____

_____

_____

_____

_____

_____

_____

_____

_____

_____

_____

_____

_____

_____

_____

_____

_____

_____

_____

_____

_____

_____

_____

_____

_____

_____

_____

CHAPTER 3

Good Girls Don't Drink, Right?

Angela

How about good *control freak* girls? Being a control freak in every sense of the phrase (just ask my friends and family), I don't understand how people can allow their minds and bodies to be altered haphazardly and without meaningful purpose by alcohol.

Fellow editor Amy Calkins writes, "I can think of plenty of good reasons to not drink alcohol, but the Bible is not one of them. Responsible drinking is within the bounds of our freedom in Christ. However, we must be ready at any moment to surrender our 'rights' according to God's specific direction: to keep another from stumbling, to embrace a fasting lifestyle, to lose weight, etc."

Search as I may, the Scriptures actually don't strictly prohibit the use of alcohol—much to my disappointment. Alcohol causes so much death, destruction of marriages, souls, and lives, senseless violence, and terrible behavior that I thought for *sure* there would be verses to substantiate my total abstinence conviction.

A dear friend's husband, J. Kenneth Long Jr., offered the (abbreviated) following:

> Several Scriptures warn against alcohol use including: Proverbs 20:1 KJV, *"Wine is a mocker, strong drink is raging, and whosoever is deceived thereby is not wise."* Proverbs 31:4b-5 KJV, *"…it is not for kings to drink wine, nor for princes strong drink, lest they drink, and forget the law, and pervert the judgment of any of the afflicted."* Proverbs 23:31-32 KJV, *"Look not thou upon the wine when it is red, when it giveth its color in the cup, when it moveth itself aright. At the last it biteth like a serpent and stingeth like an adder."* First Corinthians 6:9a,10a KJV, *"Know ye not that the unrighteousness shall not inherit the kingdom of God? Be not deceived…nor drunkards, …shall inherit the kingdom of God."* Galatians 5:19a,21b KJV, *"Now the works of the flesh are manifest, which are these: …drunkenness… that they who do such things shall not inherit the kingdom of God."*

Other Scriptures tell us how to live as Christians: Romans 12:1-2a KJV, *"I beseech you therefore, brethren, by the mercies of God, that ye present your bodies a living sacrifice, holy, acceptable unto God, which is your reasonable service. And be not conformed to this world, but be ye transformed by the renewing of your mind…"* To me, that means abstaining from certain worldly pleasures such as alcohol.

That sums it up for me as well. After all, I'm the worst backseat driver that my husband can ever attest to. And my dear daughters have had to bear the brunt of their mother being the all-time know-it-all. They all realize, though, that I am passionate about all of God's blessings and very wary of all of satan's snares.

Shae

But wouldn't how much control someone has of oneself depend on his or her alcohol tolerance level or physical makeup? I mean, an ounce or two of sherry isn't about to down Goliath, if you know what I mean. Almost everything has a "bad tag" on it, or so it seems. What *isn't* bad for us or what doesn't adversely affect us at some point. I hear what you are saying though, Angela. I'm just playing devil's advocate here. *wink* As my dear sister Woozle exclaims to me facetiously with an eye roll, *"Really* Rose!" What's a good girl to do? Can't even have a cuppa joe without someone pushing a guilt trip on me! A friend of mine, a great influential man of God and thoroughly learned in

Scripture, I might add, revealed, "Thou shalt not drink of the black bitter bean," (from Hezekiah 3:17). My narrow-but-cute jaw dropped in believable unbelief. And I thought coffee was the liquid grace of God! Happy juice, sinful? Man, did he get me! Were it not for the midriff jiggle, the circling motion of his forefinger around his temple, the silent mouthing of the word, "gullible," the thigh slapping, the eye roll, the purple face, the choking, and my smart-aleck friend's final, "I gotcha," I'd still believe I was the queen of sinners to this day! First, there is no such law, and second, there is no such book of the Bible. Ha ha. Very funny.

Of course, coffee is a sin—just as drinking alcohol, shoe collecting, and eating are sinful *if* they breach the boundaries to become gods of our heart. Can we talk? Anyone who drinks over ten café lattes a day or whose shoe closets rival those of the late Imelda Marcos needs serious revelation of *"Thou shalt have no other gods before me."* White flag flapping here in the breezes of the Canadian Pacific Northwest! Augustine put it this way, "He loves too little, who loves anything together with Thee, which he loves not for Thy sake." Then there is the stuff that causes others to stumble in a "Don't do as I do, do as I say," sense. Ever had your pastor speed past you on the highway? Talk about a double-take. Speeding, bad!

Church and its teachings are important to our spiritual growth, but most pastors agree on the importance of researching, confirming, and discovering the truth for ourselves. We truly won't believe or have faith unless our hearts hear the Truth firsthand, which is the work of the Holy Spirit speaking to us as we pray, illuminating Scripture, providing *rhema* words, in short, illuminating the path that best follows Jesus and glorifies God. This is the way I sniff out the little foxes and pranksters that get betwixt and between right and wrong to confuse me; those misguided precepts or arguments of the flesh that say, "Don't or you'll go to hell," or "Come on, Shae, one more tip of the glass won't hurt you!"

The good news is, personal revelation of the truth enables me to set my face as flint (picture too many facelifts!) toward my divine and unique purpose; and it renders possible, as Angela's colleague said, "surrender" of anything God asks of us. Try me God, but if You don't mind, can we start small, say with my thimble collection, and work our way up to, ahem, You know.

Donna

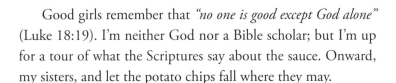

Good girls remember that *"no one is good except God alone"* (Luke 18:19). I'm neither God nor a Bible scholar; but I'm up for a tour of what the Scriptures say about the sauce. Onward, my sisters, and let the potato chips fall where they may.

Of course, biblical language becomes an issue of its own. Wine is discussed throughout the Bible. But did the word *wine* mean the same thing in ancient cultures as it does today? Not always. For us, *wine* refers strictly to an alcoholic beverage. But take, for example, Isaiah 65:8, which refers to the "new wine" found in "the [grape] cluster." The Hebrew here is *tiyrowsh,* a word overwhelmingly used to describe unfermented, fresh juice.[1] That makes sense; grape clusters yield grape juice, not wine. That said, you can't solve an issue with a single Bible verse (good girls don't do bad hermeneutics). My point is that each verse must be considered in light of cultural and historical distinctives.

Many Scriptures highlight the good cheer produced by wine. So is this an ironclad buzz endorsement? Allow me to buzz kill for a moment: the very first biblical mention of alcoholic wine use involves Noah's consequential drunkenness: *"Then he drank of the wine and was drunk…"* (Gen. 9:21). The passage goes on to describe the awful consequences of Noah's inebriation—the humiliation of Noah and the cursing of his son Canaan and Canaan's descendants. That doesn't sound like something good to me.

Then there's the miracle at Cana. (Keep your Excedrin handy.) For many, it proves Jesus' approval of alcohol use. But here's a thought-provoking question: "…Would Jesus contribute to drunkenness? …Jesus knew well the solemn warnings of Habakkuk 2:15, *'Woe to him who gives his neighbor intoxicating drink.'"*[2] Another writer offers this observation (make that two Excedrin, please): "Christ did not come to mock or deceive people, yet Proverbs 20:1 says that wine does both. Rather than coming to mock or deceive, He came to save!"[3] The Greek implies the use of alcoholic wine in John 2; but could there be more to the miracle of Cana than we understand?

Another Scripture shared by friends on both sides of the issue is Ephesians 5:18: *"Do not be drunk with wine, in which is dissipation; but be filled with the Spirit…."* Some believe this verse prohibits drunkenness, not alcohol use altogether. Others believe that being "filled" with the Spirit implies being empty of other influences. The verb meaning "be drunk" is *methusko,* which Strong's calls a "prolonged (transitive) form" of *methuo* ("to intoxicate").[4] But does the verb refer to chronic intoxication or the process of becoming drunk, which begins with the first drink?

This alcohol thing is a lot to swallow. Pass the chips. ☺

Tammy

Wow, when it comes to the Bible's words on alcohol, you ladies have it all mapped out! It seems pretty clear that there are plenty of Scriptures to condemn drunkenness and just as many that demonstrate the acceptable use, but not abuse, of alcohol. Sounds like an area for careful discernment—much trickier than if there really were a straight-up "Thou shalt not drink" in the Ten Commandments.

With that in mind, I've been studying up on the Bible's guidelines for handling Christian liberty. Galatians 5:1 NIV says, *"It is for freedom that Christ has set us free. Stand firm, then, and do not let yourselves be burdened again by a yoke of slavery."* I don't want to be a slave to alcohol, but I also don't want to return to the slavery of living under a religious law!

First Corinthians 10:23-33 stands out as a little passage with (to borrow a phrase from Donna) a lot to swallow. The tricky issue of Paul's day—eating meat that had been sacrificed to idols—sounds suspiciously akin to the controversy surrounding alcohol now. As he says, "The earth is the Lord's, and all its fullness." If I take part in the meal with thankfulness, why am I denounced because of something I thank God for? So whether you eat or drink or whatever you do, do it all for the *"glory of God"* (see 1 Cor. 10:28,31). Sounds like Paul didn't feel too convicted about issues of food and drink, and even says in verse 29 (NIV), "why should my freedom be judged by another's conscience?" Why indeed?

And yet, in the very same passage he also says, *"Do not cause anyone to stumble…even as I try to please everybody in every way. For I am not seeking my own good but the good of many, so that they may be saved"* (1 Cor. 10:32-33 NIV). A point in favor of temperance, at least! And can I just ask a question? What exactly do we mean by "not causing people to stumble"? What if I'm in the company of a person who not only feels strongly that all drinking is a sin, but also has an issue of pride and looks with condemnation on others who drink? Do I cause them to stumble by quietly following my own conscience, even if they choose to judge me for it? Or do I cause them to stumble by capitulating to their conscience and allowing their prideful attitude to pass without comment? Both? Neither? Ack!

I also admit that Paul is right: *"'Everything is permissible'—but not everything is beneficial"* (1 Cor. 10:23 NIV). And yes, "drunkenness" is one of the "obvious" sins in Galatians 5:19-21. But notice too: *"the fruit of the Spirit is love, joy, peace, patience, kindness, goodness, faithfulness, gentleness and self-control"* (Gal. 5:22-23 NIV). Hmmm…I don't see "abstinence" on this list.

Maybe that's what "self-control" means to some, but I don't think you can say that for everyone. After all, wasn't Jesus self-controlled? Yet even He drank! (See Luke 7:33-34.)

Endnotes

1. *Biblesoft's New Exhaustive Strong's Numbers and Concordance with Expanded Greek-Hebrew Dictionary.* CD-ROM. Biblesoft, Inc. and International Bible Translators, Inc. s.v. "tiyrowsh," (OT 8492).

2. "Alcohol and the Bible: New Expanded Version," *James & Dave's Bible Page,* http://www.james-dave.com/alcohol2.html (accessed July 6, 2009).

3. Bruce Lackey, *What the Bible Teaches About Drinking Wine* (Chattanooga: Bruce Lackey, 1985), 13.

4. Strong's, s.v. "methusko," (NT 3182).

Your Reflections

_____

_____

_____

_____

_____

_____

_____

_____

_____

_____

_____

_____

Your Reflections

_____

_____

_____

_____

_____

_____

_____

_____

_____

_____

_____

_____

_____

_____

_____

_____

_____

_____

_____

_____

_____

_____

_____

_____

_____

_____

_____

_____

Your Reflections

_____

_____

_____

_____

_____

_____

_____

_____

_____

_____

_____

_____

_____

_____

_____

_____

_____

_____

_____

_____

_____

_____

_____

_____

_____

_____

_____

_____

_____

_____

_____

_____

_____

Chapter 4

Messages From the Busch

Shae

The map is in my heart, Tammy. And I wish I'd had the truth of God's Word etched there a long time ago! I did not become a responsible drinker overnight! Alarmingly, I first learned moderation through the consequences of over-drinking and *not* by way of conviction, example, warnings, the Word, or safe drinking messages. Golly gee, I grew up in the golden age of the cocktail hour where parents shuffled kids to bed, turned on the jazz, plunked their olives into martini glasses, and lit up their smokes. The Cleavers drank. Uncle Bill drank. The Bradys drank. That Girl drank. Mr.

and Mrs. Thirsten Howell the Third drank. Dean Martin drank.

I had my first "adult" drink, a vodka screwdriver, as a young teen, and I knew nothing about "easy does it," nor did my friends. It was "all or nothing," and we finished the bottle, a 40-pounder, in one setting. Ugh. I passed out for almost 48 hours, and had a one-week hangover. But teens tend to do everything to the extreme in the company of friends, and alcohol is no exception, which may be why binge drinking is a top social woe today, and why the responsible drinking placards the alcohol industry raises are of little effect, and why young people make good customers. ('K, breathe Shae). The result, millions of binge-drinking adults, and untold alcohol-related poisonings and deaths. Ever notice how the ads feature four or more people? Wherever people gather seems always an excuse or stimulus for a gallon of something. Alcohol is made to look fun, as a social must, and even as a way to relax from life pressures, and this renders most warnings mute. I venture the industry even does psychological profiling. Do you know that you will never see a woman drink alcohol out of a brown glass in a television commercial?

Parents, teachers, pastors, and leaders are scrambling to figure out ways to deflect the industry's feel-good missiles, which seem even to penetrate the physical and spiritual hedges we proactively place around our loved ones. Does the industry *really care* enough about our youth, or people for that matter, to genuinely and with as much effort as they expend for the mighty buck, promote responsible use of or, where merited, abstinence from alcohol?

Is the answer to just stop advertising alcohol? The message is still "Drink up," albeit a little more desperate in light of increasing pressures lobbying against in-your-face advertising. The tobacco industry in its last days, appeared to beef up its behind-the-scene strategies: Distract public debate, steer clear of negative attention, schmooze the medical profession, avoid damaging policies, appeal psychologically, get lots of sponsorship, lobby against advertising restrictions, regulatory controls, and tax hikes, lobby for lowering the legal age, guerrilla market the gullible, the easily swayed, and the up and comers. I have a problem with these tactics, particularly since they seem to work to the tune of $23 billion a year to the alcohol industry courtesy of underage drinkers—over 17 percent of all money spent on alcohol in the United States.[1] Nothing moderate there! Now, here's a shocker—50 percent of all of the revenues came in by way of the underage and *adults* who abused alcohol—irresponsible drinkers. Alcohol abusers are their best customers!

If my father were alive and drinking as much as he did before he joined AA, that revenue stat would soar to 75 percent! I think the local grocer retired on what he made from my father in beer revenue. Now while Dad certainly made his own choices, Mr. Dumas had choices, too. Did he care that Ernie had seven hungry mouths to feed? That he would stagger home to abuse his wife? That he would lose his job and only source of income? That Mom was sick and needed help? That his client's children were on the streets in the middle of winter bootless? Did he direct my father to a source of help for his addiction? Did he choose not to serve him? No, but he did gladly run my father a tab and beat the door down when it went three months overdue. I have to think that caring choices begin at the top, and believe that they filter down.

Angela

The Cleavers drank? Say it isn't so! I must have missed that episode. Yes, Shae, you're right about what the alcohol industry has to say…Bottoms Up! And, of course, it has the same mantra as the tobacco and gun companies, "We just sell the stuff, we don't make them drink it, smoke it, shoot it, blah, blah, blah." Yeah, right.

Well, tell that to "poor" Tiger Woods who was heckled during a golf tournament on June 20, 2009, by drunken fans. Newsday.com reported that a dozen "beer-sodden fans" taunted Woods as he prepared to start his third round. "We're on Long Island, baby, where men are men! Put that umbrella down!" Woods didn't respond to the hecklers but tried to quiet them with a "shhh." The drunks responded with, "Suck it up, you've got your own video game!" Earlier, drunken fans at the seventh hole shouted, "This Bud's for you!" On the ninth fairway, drunks called out, "You suck," to players while spectators on the other side booed the hecklers.

Would these men have been so rude if not for the beers they were gulping? I think not. Well, I hope not. And how about the football games and NASCAR races that are enjoyable for some, but not for those who find themselves sitting beside a group of drunks who are loud and obnoxious? Why do people drink while attending a favorite sporting event? The action would be less intense, their senses dulled. And if they drank too much, they wouldn't even remember what happened.

And tell that to our youth. Join Together, an organization that advances effective alcohol and drug policy, prevention, and treatment, posted on its Web site an interesting article about the alcohol industry and our children. Portions follow:

> …no one spends more money to get through to teens about drinking than the alcohol industry itself.

> Alcohol companies encourage youth to drink by using kid-friendly content in their advertisements, such as cartoons, humor, or music, and by implying that having fun and being attractive means drinking alcohol. In fact, the industry targets teens so aggressively that underage children see more alcohol ads in magazines than adults do.

> More difficult to monitor than advertising, however, is the unmeasured multi-billion dollar a year practice of alcohol promotion. Companies design promotions to expose underage children to positive messages about alcohol, by means of trendy logo apparel, discounts to appeal to price-sensitive youth, and sponsorship of youth culture activities such as concerts and sporting events.

> There is also new research indicating that alcohol, tobacco, and illicit drugs act differently on adolescent

brains as they are growing than they do on fully mature brains. For some, early use of alcohol, tobacco, and illicit drugs may actually change brain development in long-lasting and detrimental ways.

Of course, you should always consider the source of any report or statistics that you read, but this group obviously has our young people's best interests at heart. Can the alcohol industry say the same?

Donna

"Our message to kids [about alcohol] is, 'we'll wait for your business,' says Bill."[2]

If I had kids, I'd be all about that kind of advice, dontcha know. But holy Rocky Mountain High, you won't believe who's giving it. It's Bill Young, a Molson Coors' exec. Yup—you read that right. Coors spends money to drive down beer sales (albeit much of this revenue would have been from underaged youths whose participation is discouraged only temporarily).

Apparently, this has been Young's mission for years. In the 1990s, he was the executive director of a substance abuse prevention program for the state of Colorado. Now he works for a manufacturer of alcoholic beverages. "Come again?" you query.

What I said was, "Honey (that's a generic, unromantic "honey," BTW), you'd better balance your brewski and get a scorecard if you want to keep up with this roster." Bill Young isn't any old executive; he's Molson Coors' Director of Corporate Responsibility. According to the company, he's "fighting the causes of harmful drinking from within the Coors Brewing Company."[3]

OK, that's weird. Maybe it's not a full-fledged moment of incredulity, but you'll grant me that it's downright ironic, right? Gone are the days when you can sell beer with a clear head, however oxymoronic that concept may be. In our PC, PR-driven, litigious twentieth-first-century, beer selling is an enigmatic venture. You've got to beat your competitors and protect (or at least look like you're protecting) the nation's youth and all vulnerable populations from demon alcohol (a good, but somewhat impossible task).

I'm guessing the Coors Marketing Department is on the opposite end of the building from Bill Young's office. But, helloooooooo, Coors' primary mission is to sell beer. Anheuser Busch, Heineken, and any other beer company has the same goal. The Marin Institute speaks pointedly to this side of the Coors mission saying, "Despite its own assertions that Coors 'will not condone underage drinking,' the third largest brewer is spending hundreds of thousands of dollars on advertising that is guaranteed to reach millions of youth."[4]

Let me just say that I'm not judging Coors or Bill Young; they are conducting a legal enterprise according to the laws of the land. And I commend their outreach efforts. But the issue is necessarily tied up in cross-purposes. So is their message. I've seen their ads; I'm pretty sure they want me—and some *much* younger folks—to buy a lot of beer. (Am I misreading their commercials???) Sure, I have an opinion or two about youth, alcohol, and exploitation, but this chapter isn't about me or my opinions. It's about what the alcohol industry says, which, for the most part is, "Drink up."

No surprise there. Beer has been around for millennia. It's brewed to bring pleasure to consumers and mammon to producers.

This is a fallen world, after all.

Tammy

Right you are, Donna—it's a business, they're selling a product, and naturally, their main message is going to be "Drink!" as you have all pointed out. But I'd say the alcohol industry easily goes a step farther than that, anticipating the number-one question any two-year-old will ask when given an ultimatum: "Why?"

Their advertising makes it pretty clear why—identity. The same thing that drives advertising for jeans, cars, yes, even shoes! The company isn't just selling you a pair of pumps or a brand of booze—it is selling you an identity that you can have, hold, and wear on your sleeve for the world to see.

Bud Light claims that "The difference is drinkability," but it would be more accurate to say that the difference is in how you want to see yourself. Captain Morgan rum shows commercials where comical fellows pull off smooth moves in a pinch and win with the ladies…and, "They got a little Captain in them. Got a little Captain in you?" And if you're a real down-home American soul with a fondness for grass-roots tradition, everything about the image of Jack Daniel's whiskey is geared to appeal to you. Then again, you might aspire to more international flavor in your life. Tanqueray gin says, "Resist simple," and paints images of confident, cosmopolitan young adults. (Gotta be honest—this one does a good job appealing to me.) And of course, absolutely every brand and brew—from wine to beer to the whole spectrum of hard liquors—is a guaranteed *huge* boost to your sex appeal.

So they tell us.

And of course, once again, the identity-mongering messages the alcohol industry sends through its advertising are essentially not that different from the culture of materialism in general. But I'm also listening to a higher voice—one that says I already have an identity, before and above all others. I am the Lord's, designed and directed by Him, here on earth to do His work (see Eph. 2:10).

So maybe Bacardi is "Alive with taste." But they should try "life by the Spirit." Good stuff. ^_^

Endnotes

1. May 2, 2006, Reuters article concerning a report by researches from New York's Columbia University.

2. "MVParents.com: Involved Parents Are the Real Heroes," Molson Coors, http://www.molsoncoors.

com/responsibility/product-responsibility/alcohol-responsibility/initiatives/mvparents (accessed July 12, 2009).

3. Ibid.

4. "Alcohol Advertising Alert: Coors Targeting Youth," The Marin Institute, http://www.marininstitute.org/alcohol_industry/ad_alerts/coors.htm (accessed, July 12, 2009).

Your Reflections

_____

_____

_____

_____

_____

_____

_____

_____

_____

_____

_____

_____

_____

_____

_____

_____

_____

_____

_____

_____

_____

_____

_____

_____

_____

_____

_____

_____

_____

_____

_____

_____

_____

_____

_____

_____

_____

_____

_____

_____

_____

_____

_____

_____

_____

_____

_____

_____

_____

_____

_____

_____

_____

_____

_____

_____

_____

_____

_____

Chapter 5

Rx or XXX?

Angela

My big brother (a retired Marine Corps officer) may have answered the question to why I have such strong anti-alcohol feelings. When I queried his opinion about drinking, his reply was, "Christ turned water into wine. Why? Because the waters flowing over most of this earth even then were contaminated. A little alcohol, from grain to beer; or from fruit to wine, killed some of the germs. A little red wine is good for circulation."

BUT THEN I had to read the next sentence several times

before it sunk in, "And by the way, our mother drank one can of beer per day for a few weeks on the doctor's orders while carrying you some time before you were born." What?! Are you kidding me?!

In fact, that's what I e-mailed back to him. What?! Are you kidding me?! As far as I knew, our mother never drank *any* alcohol beverages. Ever. She was 40 years old when I was born, though, so maybe the doctor figured that she needed an extra boost of "atta girl" to get her through my pre-born antics?

That was 54 years ago; today the "experts" discourage drinking alcohol during pregnancy, as it is linked to a higher risk of cancers. Kathleen Doheny on WebMD.com writes that "researchers found that women who had as little as one drink a day boosted their risk of cancer of the breast, liver, rectum, throat, mouth, and esophagus. Meanwhile, numerous studies dating back decades show that alcohol and heart health have a positive relationship."

Ummm, that sounds more like a political campaign speech than solid medical evidence. Another example, "There's no one answer; it has to be individualized according to the specific person," says Arthur Klatsky, M.D., a former practicing cardiologist and now an investigator for Kaiser Permanente. "The research on alcohol's effect on health suggests both harm and benefits," says Gary Rogg, M.D., an internal medicine specialist at Montefiore Medical Center and assistant professor and assistant director of the department of internal medicine at Albert Einstein College of Medicine, New York. "The studies show links to breast cancer [and] links to liver cancer [with alcohol intake]," he says, as well as to other cancers. "If you reduce alcohol intake you can reduce the incidence of head and neck cancer and colorectal cancer. Having said that, there seems to be a benefit with [alcohol] and heart disease."

My expert medical advice? Make an appointment with the Great Physician. His prognosis and advice is *always* correct—and prescribed especially for you!

Shae

Oh, I love the prognosis: a new, transformed, eternally 18-year-old healthy body. Wine improves with age—oh that my figure would, too! As I approach 50 and well into the fermentation cycle of life, it is hard enough to maintain this temple of the Holy Spirit wherein I serve God while trying to keep everything "up," if you know what I mean. Thank goodness for grace, and for padded push-up bras, uh, again, if you know what I mean!

Fermenting wine produces gas, did you know that? Job did. He said, "The wind in my belly presses me. My belly is like wine not yet opened like jugs of new wine ready to burst." Now, he said this in the context of having a whole lot to say, *"I am full of words…let me speak, then, let me open my lips and reply"* (Job 32:18-20, Jewish Study Bible). Having something to say is as good an excuse for a fluff if ever I heard one!

God's advice *is* spot on! He obligates us to *nourish* and *cherish* our bodies (see Eph. 5:29), but oh, my morning face lends credence to the saying, "She has a face only a mother could love." Moreover, the Bible says that our bodies are God's handiwork, and should inspire awe of His glorious, marvelous, creative power. I take that to mean, without exception. The face looking back at me in the mirror inspires "ugh," some days, which BTW is a total breach of the command for older women not to be enslaved to too much whine…or is that "wine?" (see Titus 2:3). Should be both!

Who hath woe? Who hath sorrow? Who hath contentions? Who hath babbling? Who hath wounds without cause? Who hath redness of eyes? According to Proverbs 23:29-32, people who tarry *long* at wine. This is dead right, medically speaking! Indeed, the person with "red eyes" *and* sallow skin and puffy face likely drinks too much, according to *Beautiful Skin: Every Woman's Guide to Looking Her Best at Any Age*.[1] Experts agree that alcohol dehydrates the body at the cellular level so it also contributes to (horror!) wrinkles! *Medline Plus*, an online service of the *U.S. National Library of Medicine* and the *National Institutes of Health*, and, the *Encyclopedia of Alcoholism* cite all sorts of indirect physical (wounds without a cause) and emotional (woe, sorrow, contentions, babbling) ailments as a result of alcohol dependence and abuse.

For instance, the binge drinker is prone to vomiting, which can lead to agitation of or bleeding of the esophagus. Overdrinking can cause brain degeneration and depression. They agree that moderate drinking for those not in the high risk categories—(alcoholics, children, pregnant women, people on certain medicines and people with some medical conditions)—is probably safe and may even have health benefits, including reducing the risk of certain heart problems, though the subject is still controversial. The National Institute on Alcohol Abuse and Alcoholism recommends women have no more than one drink (12 oz. bottle of beer, 5 oz. glass of wine, or 1.5 oz. shot of liquor) per day and men no more than two drinks per day. Wrinkle wise, moderation sure beats undergoing a $10,000 facelift. I'm good with that!

Donna

What do medical experts say about alcohol? Depends on the day—uh—make that *the study*. Short of doing a new study (oooohhh, that could be a dangerous bit of sampling), I thought I'd sample some expert opinions instead:

"Moderate drinkers tend to have better health and live longer than those who are either abstainers or heavy drinkers. In addition to having fewer heart attacks and strokes, moderate consumers of alcoholic beverages (beer, wine or distilled spirits or liquor) are generally less likely to suffer hypertension or high blood pressure, peripheral artery disease, Alzheimer's disease and the common cold. Sensible drinking also appears to be beneficial in reducing or preventing diabetes, rheumatoid arthritis, bone fractures…"[2]

Hold it right there! You mean moderate drinkers have a healthy leg up on abstainers? Apparently, the laundry list of preventative benefits goes on and on. Makes a "dry" gal consider popping the cork! (But will a good Pinot grigio keep me healthy *and* clean my windows?) Another click of the mouse says, "Not so fast, sista: 'Drinking alcohol can cause cancer. Research shows that men who have two alcoholic drinks a day and women who have one alcoholic drink a day have an increased chance of developing certain cancers.'"[3]

Yo—who just moved my cheese? Where did all those benefits go? Click. Looks like they moved to the Mediterranean: "Moderate alcohol intake may be the single biggest contributor to the Mediterranean diet's longevity benefit, accounting for 23.5% of the effect in a prospective cohort study."[4] No wonder my grandfather lived to see his 95th birthday!

But just when I think I've got this thing figured, here comes a downer for our East Asian friends: "It is very important for clinicians who treat patients of East Asian descent to be aware of the risk of esophageal cancer from alcohol consumption in their patients who exhibit the alcohol flushing response [an enzyme deficiency that causes reddening of the face], so they can counsel them about limiting their drinking…"[5] Back to the drawing board.

You get my not-so-medical drift. Expert opinions are based on so many studies of so many groups with so many predispositions and practices and/or concurrent indulgences (hellooo—Mediterraneans also eat the magic oil of the olive and eat less meat; while many regular consumers of alcohol are also regular smokers…yada, yada—or, as Shae would say—Prada, Prada) it's a little hard to tell the causes from the effects.

Is this as clear as mud, yet?

Tammy

I don't think I've ever heard a medical opinion in favor of excessive drinking. Nobody's silly enough to say that alcoholism or drunkenness are good for what ails ya. And I think it's pretty much a given that too much alcohol is only damaging to health. That's a no-brainer, and anyone who argues that point needs their head checked—with the business end of a wet noodle.

What's more, it's clear that there are a few additional medical reasons to lay off the lager. Certain conditions—like that East Asian condition you mentioned, Donna—as well as things like a family history of alcoholism, having a weak liver, or being pregnant can all affect an individual's choice to drink. Hopefully those who have such medical reasons not to drink will also have the wisdom to abstain. Especially pregnant mothers—please, think of the children!

Personally, I feel that these are examples of situations where the medical opinion rightly warns us off the cocktails, and smart cookies will find their match in a glass of milk, not a martini. However, for the rest of us, provided we keep our intake moderate, there are quite a few health benefits from a little wine, beer, or even liquor. Boston University School of Medicine's Dr. Curtis Ellison says, "Study after study has shown that moderate consumers of beer or other alcoholic beverages have much lower risks of coronary heart disease, as well as most other diseases of aging."[6]

What are some of these other diseases of aging that alcohol can help with? How about hypertension, high blood pressure, peripheral artery disease, Alzheimer's disease, the common cold, diabetes, rheumatoid arthritis, bone fractures, osteoporosis, kidney stones, digestive problems, stress, depression, poor cognition and memory, Parkinson's disease, hepatitis A, pancreatic cancer, macular degeneration (a big contributor to blindness), angina pectoris, duodenal ulcers, erectile dysfunction, hearing loss, gallstones, and liver disease.[7] Quite a list, huh?

For a final surprise, studies show that those who drink moderately—no more than one drink a day for women and two for men—actually tend to live longer than heavy drinkers *and* abstainers alike![8] Shocker! I wonder if that's because abstainers' risk of stroke is twice that of moderate drinkers?[9]

Before anyone gets the idea that alcohol is a new cure-all miracle treatment, I should add that all of these studies were of drinkers and abstainers who lived very healthy lifestyles in general. So if you're looking to justify your boozing with a doctor's say-so—sorry, it's a no-go. However, for those genuinely interested in improving their health, who are taking active steps in other areas of their lives (and, remember, who aren't at risk for some other reason)—tip your glass to moderation!

After all, even Paul counseled Timothy: *"Stop drinking only water, and use a little wine because of your stomach and your frequent illnesses"* (1 Tim. 5:23 NIV).

Endnotes

1. *Beautiful Skin: Every Woman's Guide to Looking Her Best at Any Age* (David E. Bank, Estelle Sobel; Pub. Adams Media), May 1, 2000.

2. "Alcohol Problems and Solutions, 'Alcohol and Health,'" University of Potsdam, NY, http://www2.potsdam.edu/hansondj/alcoholandhealth.html (accessed July 19, 2009).

3. "Alcohol and Cancer," American Cancer Society, http://www.cancer.org/downloads/PRO/alcohol.pdf 2006 (accessed July 19, 2009).

4. Crystal Phend, "Alcohol Top 'Active Ingredient' in Mediterranean Diet" "June 24, 2009," *MedPage Today,* http://www.medpagetoday.com/PrimaryCare/DietNutrition/14843 (accessed July 19, 2009).

5. "Alcohol Flush Signals Increased Cancer Risk among East Asians," *NIH News,* (March 23, 2009), http://www.nih.gov/news/health/mar2009/niaaa-23.htm (accessed July 19, 2009).

6. http://www.nutraingredients-usa.com/Research/Studies-uphold-health-benefits-of-alcohol).

7. http://www2.potsdam.edu/hansondj/alcoholandhealth.html.

8. Ibid.

9. H. Rodgers et al. "A case-control study of drinking habits past and present." *Stroke*, 1993, 24(10), 1473-1477.

Your Reflections

_____

_____

_____

_____

_____

_____

_____

_____

_____

_____

_____

_____

_____

_____

_____

_____

_____

_____

_____

_____

_____

_____

_____

_____

_____

_____

_____

_____

_____

_____

_____

_____

_____

_____

_____

_____

_____

_____

_____

_____

_____

_____

_____

_____

_____

_____

_____

_____

_____

_____

_____

_____

_____

_____

_____

_____

_____

_____

_____

CHAPTER 6

What "They" Say

Shae

Is it me, Tam, or am I wrong in noticing that more and more Christians…and dare I say Charismatics, seem to be "trying to stay healthy" these days? There is hardly a dry spot anywhere, and I wonder. There does seem a rise in drinking within the Body of Christ at large too, which could present problems because moderate drinkers do occasionally drink at high-risk levels, according to the World Health Organization (WHO).

I agree. A little bit of alcohol is good, but very quickly a little more becomes bad—way bad. Once the introduction to alcohol is made, the affair usually flourishes on its own. As George Burns used to say, "It takes only one drink to get me drunk. The trouble is, I can't remember if it's the thirteenth or the fourteenth!" In the past, the temptation to have another drink and even another sometimes was just too great for me, particularly with a good vintage table side, in the heat of summer, in a party/holiday atmosphere, under stress, while emotionally deplete, or with a generously pushy host constantly topping off my drink even over my objections. Tipsy blonde Christians, not good! The morning after I would have to deal, as Jimmy Breslin, the American journalist put it, "with this marvelous personality that started [me] drinking in the first place." Today, I do not make the mistakes I used to, but it is hard to cultivate *consistent* self-control, which Proverbs 4:23 describes as keeping our hearts with all diligence, which is key for everything we will face.

No one sets out to become an alcoholic, to be sure. I don't want to be the one to put the grape in a urine sample, if you know what I mean, but the risk *is* there for some people. Thankfully, I am not alcohol dependent, and rarely drink nowadays because my body wants to upchuck at times. Can you say, "Ralph?" Good thing too because *"He that hath no rule over his own spirit is like a city that is broken down, and without walls"* (Prov. 25:28 KJV). I do have a Spirit-dependency, though, and overindulge regularly! But it is worth becoming one's own organization (of course, placing God as CEO), and scrutinizing ourselves and asking (before tipping the bubbly), "Am I good to go, God? Are my walls up? Am I at risk? Am I in control? Do I have the character/maturity/emotional mind-set to say no all the time to the one-too-many?"

Angela

George Burns, eh? I vaguely remember him, Shae—you must be way older than I am. ;) Or maybe you're just a classic comic fan?

Anyway, almost 99 percent of the friends, family, pastors, neighbors, and colleagues I polled agree with the "moderation" line of thinking. Some even wrote "**everything** in moderation." Ummm, really? Does that include lying? Cheating? Road rage? Theft? Using illegal drugs? Pornography? Child molestation? Rape? Murder? I think not. We must place restrictions on ourselves (with the help of our heavenly Father) that ensure a civil society, a productive community, a healthy family.

MADD, Mothers Against Drunk Driving, was founded in 1980, and its mission is to stop drunk driving, support the victims of this violent crime, and prevent underage drinking. MADD's Web site is full of tragic statistics that are anything but moderate, including:

- Almost 13,000 people died because of drunk drivers in 2007.
- 32% of all traffic deaths were caused by drunk drivers in 2007.
- A drunk driver has driven drunk 87 times prior to being arrested the first time.
- 50-75% of drunk drivers who have had their licenses suspended continue to drive.
- More than 1.46 million drivers were arrested

in 2006 who were under the influence of alcohol or narcotics.

- 40% of people convicted of violent crimes were drinking at the time of the event.

- On average, a person is killed every 40 minutes because of a drunk driver.

- In 2001, on average, a person was injured every minute in an alcohol-related incident—500,000 people.

- $1.9 billion was spent on beer, wine, and liquor advertising in the United States, 10 times more than for milk.

Check out www.madd.org for more shocking information about how drinking and driving destroys millions of lives each year.

SADD, Students Against Drunk Driving, was founded in 1981, and the mission is to provide students with the best prevention tools possible to deal with the issues of underage drinking, other drug use, impaired driving, and other destructive decisions. More than 350,000 students across the country are members of this organization aimed at keeping their classmates alive.

A few statistics found at www.sadd.org are from a 2005 survey that revealed:

- 10.8 million young people (ages 12-20) under the legal age to drink alcohol reported drinking within the past month.

- 7.2 million young people (ages 12-20) are binge drinkers.
- 2.3 million young people (ages 12-20) were heavy drinkers.
- 41% of students have consumed alcohol (more than a few sips) by 8th grade.

Family environment has a significant effect on young people's views about alcohol consumption. In this, I agree with "moderation." Colleague Kathy Deering wrote that, "One of my grandmothers was a member of the WCTU (Women's Christian Temperance Union). A vehement teetotaler, she did not endear herself, or her other Christian beliefs, to her six children. As a result, none of them were Christians until very late in their lives, and they consciously rebelled against her principles. Therefore, I grew up in a home where alcohol beverages were served on special occasions (except when Grandma came to visit!). When I became a Christian in my early teens, I began to realize that Christians had more "issues" with alcohol than I had thought—and they had issues with each other on account of it."

Donna

When I was growing up, there was a woman up the block who had several children. I remember her being pregnant and walking "to the stores" with her kids, cigarette in hand. Nothing unusual there. In those days, lots of moms, pregnant and otherwise, smoked with the brood in tow and one in the oven.

The unusual piece, in my juvenile mind, was the fact that this woman had an alcohol problem and drank her way through her pregnancy. I'm not sure how I learned this; perhaps I overheard my parents talking about it as I sneaked out of bed to catch a past-my-bedtime glimpse of "Dr. Kildare."

I do remember learning that my mom and others were worried about this woman's condition. Nevertheless, the drinking allegedly continued and the child was born seemingly without complication. In time, however, she proved to be developmentally disabled.

The suspicion among the neighbors was that alcohol had contributed to the child's condition. The correlation was seen as taboo at the time. Today, the child's condition would have a name: *fetal alcohol syndrome* or *fetal alcohol spectrum disorders* ("…an umbrella term describing the range of effects that can occur in an individual whose mother drank alcohol during pregnancy"[1]).

"Fetal alcohol syndrome (FAS) is a set of physical and mental birth defects that can result when a woman drinks alcohol during her pregnancy. When a pregnant woman drinks alcohol, such as beer, wine, or mixed drinks, so does her baby. Alcohol passes through the placenta right into the developing baby. The baby may suffer lifelong damage as a result."[2]

Here are some statistics, courtesy of the National Organization on Fetal Alcohol Syndrome:

- FASD is the leading known preventable cause of mental retardation and birth defects.

- FASD affects 1 in 100 live births or as many as 40,000 infants each year.…

- Children do not outgrow FASD. The physical and behavioral problems can last for a lifetime.…

- FAS and FASD are not genetic disorders. Women with FAS or affected by FASD have healthy babies if they do not drink alcohol during their pregnancy.[3]

The stats tell a powerful story. In my mind, a blunt scientific statement closes the argument: "Fetal death is the most extreme outcome"[4] of alcohol use by a pregnant woman. Thankfully, our neighbor's child survived gestation. She did, however, pay the price for her mother's addiction. I imagine she is still paying the price.

Tammy

I tried to get a statement on alcohol consumption from my favorite restaurant—the waiter brought me the wine menu. I asked at my favorite department store next. They gave me a funny look and said as long as I didn't vomit on their floor or bother the other customers, they wouldn't kick me out. Clearly, my investigation was heading in the wrong direction, LOL.

Cheers to the Internet! Here are a few statements taken from some organization Web sites:

The Beer Institute and its members continue to

implement dozens of national and community-based education and awareness programs to combat illegal underage drinking, drunk driving, and alcohol abuse. These kinds of efforts…have produced results. According to research conducted by the federal government and academic institutions, there have been declines in drunk-driving fatalities and underage drinking for more than 25 years. *(Sure, everyone scoffed over those assemblies in high school, but I guess some of us were listening after all. I know I was!)*

The people hurt most by drugs and alcohol don't even use them; they are the *children* of alcoholics and other drug-dependent parents. The National Association for Children of Alcoholics (NACoA) believes that none of these vulnerable children should grow up in isolation and without support. Our mission is to…help kids hurt by parental alcohol and drug use. It's the innocent children (1 in 4 under the age of 18) who suffer when their parents abuse alcohol and other drugs. *(These guys have my support, 100 percent. No child should have to suffer for a parent's lack of self-control.)*

The consumption of wine, beer, and spirits is an integral part of normal life in virtually all societies. As the world becomes ever more integrated, the industry faces differing and often competing views of the proper place of alcohol beverages in society because, as with many other choices in life, there are benefits and risks. While the scientific evidence of the healthful benefits of moderate consumption continues to mount, FIVS [the International Federation of Wines and Spirits] also recognizes that excessive consumption can be harmful. To that end, FIVS encourages appropriate and responsible enjoyment by those who choose to consume alcohol beverage products." *(Hey, if they do nothing else, at least this organization talks sense! LOL.)*

Women for Sobriety is an organization whose purpose is to help all women recover from problem drinking through the discovery of self gained by sharing experiences, hopes, and encouragement with other women in similar circumstances. Women for Sobriety believes that drinking began to overcome stress, loneliness, frustration, emotional deprivation, or any number of other kinds of harassment. Dependence and addiction resulted. This physiological addiction can only be overcome by abstinence. Mental and emotional addiction are overcome with the knowledge of self. *(I know Someone else who can help them with that too—His Spirit of perfect love can drive out all fear and lack!)*

There are organizations galore working to combat alcoholism and drunkenness, and it doesn't take a "dry" society to put most of them out of work. Just that last fruit of the Spirit—self-control. If everyone could learn to live controlled lives and drink in moderation, the alcohol industry could stay in business, but Alcoholics Anonymous could close its doors!

Endnotes

1. "Fetal Alcohol Spectrum Disorders," Centers for Disease Control and Prevention, (May 2, 2006), http://www.cdc.gov/ncbddd/FAS/fasask.htm (accessed July 27, 2009).

2. National Organization on Fetal Alcohol Syndrome, "What Is FAS/FASD?" http://www.nofas.org/faqs.aspx?id=9 (accessed July 27, 2009).

3. National Organization on Fetal Alcohol Syndrome, "What Are the Statistics and Facts about FAS and FASD?" http://www.nofas.org/faqs.aspx?id=12 (accessed July 27, 2009).

4. Centers for Disease Control and Prevention, Ibid.

Your Reflections

_____

_____

_____

_____

_____

_____

_____

_____

_____

_____

_____

_____

_____

_____

_____

_____

_____

_____

_____

_____

_____

_____

_____

_____

_____

_____

_____

Your Reflections

_____

_____

_____

_____

_____

_____

_____

_____

_____

_____

_____

_____

_____

_____

_____

_____

_____

_____

_____

_____

_____

_____

_____

_____

_____

_____

_____

_____

_____

_____

CHAPTER 7

Stats, Anyone?

Shae

Grrr to Angela on the age dig. I may heat my tea with my hot flashes and my son may think I co-authored the Dead Sea Scrolls, but I am still young! Yo, Angela. Did you ever find the purse you left on Noah's Ark? LOL!

Hey. I am not one for mining lengthy statistics, especially when they stare us in the face. Most of us know of an alcoholic, read the headlines, or have witnessed or even fallen victim to an alcohol-induced crime, misdemeanor, or tragedy. We have seen the disastrous effects of the killer cocktail: car, people, and alcohol. We know families torn apart by abusive alcoholics. Shelters full and overloaded with women and children in hiding appeal to us for more funds. Alcohol factored in the fate of almost every foster child I met while growing up as a suitcase kid myself. Reality cop shows usually result in the arrest of someone under the influence of alcohol. Every year, we hear of students dying in college dorms from alcohol poisoning. Faith wanes at the fall of church leaders. Sure enough, alcohol threads its way through whatever the reason for their moral demise. Carnage abounds, yes, even in the last bastion sanctuaries of church and Christian homes. The stresses and strains evidently are taking their toll on us, and we are paying the cost dearly in the unraveling of family and moral fabric.

There just does not seem to be one place left that our abusive tendencies in many things do not infiltrate, even overindulging in good things, for goodness' sake! Over and above alcohol, drugs, and other matters, our *worst habit* is our tendency to allow harmful things to get out of hand before we expend effort to curtail them. Why? Some say because of our reluctance to breach personal freedoms. But this has resulted in a nation bound in a death grip called "Take your own chances, pay your own dues, or have others pay for you." Are individual liberties worth it? Are individual liberties concerning sexual promiscuity worth STDs and AIDS outbreaks? Are individual liberties concerning a woman's right to abortion worth the killing of millions of innocents, possibly our great leaders and influencers of tomorrow? Are individual liberties concerning alcohol worth the death of even one teen son or daughter; the homelessness of even one child or adult? And, most importantly, are individual liberties worth the loss of even one soul for our God, who wills that not even one should perish, but have *everlasting life* with Him, and life most abundantly?

Yes, I am a moderationist, but I also am for a dry personal and national culture and even giving up and banning the use of alcohol if it means we can help anyone overcome the elements in their daily lives that cause them to use alcohol as an anesthesia to endure or escape the pain and agony of whatever binds them and direct them to true healing, freedom, and escapism, found only in the Person of Jesus who displaces every craving and every need, including the need for personal freedom, with LOVE. From that lofty platform of grace comes the greatest and highest freedoms.

Angela

Ummm…I found that purse, Shae. Didn't you see me on Antiques Roadshow—it's worth a fortune now! :)

As a former newspaper reporter and current on-frequent-occasion researcher, I'm all into mining for facts, figures, and the story behind the story. Digging through reports, surveys, books, articles, libraries, and surfing the Web are natural highs for me. Yea, I know, I'm weird. But God created meat and potatoes people as well as veggies and fruits. Ummm…change that to cotton and loafer-wearing women as well as silk and stiletto-wearing women. Anyway, I'll try and present them in a way that won't make your eyes glaze over and your head hurt.

What do tough, ready-to-defend Army soldiers and Marines have in common with innocent, unable-to-defend-themselves unborn babies? Alcohol abuse.

From a *USA Today* June 19, 2009, article by Gregg Zoroya,

> The rate of Army soldiers enrolled in treatment programs for alcohol dependency or abuse has nearly doubled since 2003—a sign of the growing stress of repeated deployments in Iraq and Afghanistan, according to Army statistics and interviews. …Likewise, Marines who screen positive for drug or alcohol problems increased 12% from 2005 to 2008, according to Marine Corps statistics. In addition, there were 1,060 drunken-driving cases involving Marines during the first seven months of fiscal 2009, which began in October, compared with 1,430 cases in all of fiscal 2008. …Chiarelli said identifying and treating substance and alcohol abuse will help improve the Army's mental health care and curb suicides, which reached a record 142 cases in 2008. There have been 82 confirmed or suspected suicides this year among active-duty, compared with 51 for the same period in 2008.

As Shae and Donna mentioned, and according to the MayoClinic.org:

> Fetal alcohol syndrome is a condition that results from prenatal alcohol exposure. The defects that are part of fetal alcohol syndrome are irreversible and can include serious physical, mental and behavioral

problems, though they vary from one child to another. As many as 40,000 babies are born with some type of alcohol-related damage each year in the United States.

Soldiers and babies suffer from the effects of alcohol. Lives dedicated to securing and preserving freedoms are in bondage; pure little bodies are being damaged even before taking their first breath of fresh air. [heavy sigh]

Headlines read: Hard Economic Times. Highest Unemployment Rates in Decades. Slow Economy. Mortgages and Credit Card Bills Unpaid. Yet "Americans spend over $90 billion total on alcohol each year. An average American may consume over 25 gallons of beer, 2 gallons of wine, and 1.5 gallons of distilled spirits each year," according to DrugRehabs.org.

Where are our priorities?

Donna

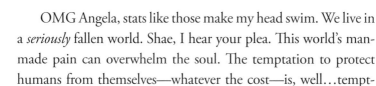

OMG Angela, stats like those make my head swim. We live in a *seriously* fallen world. Shae, I hear your plea. This world's man-made pain can overwhelm the soul. The temptation to protect humans from themselves—whatever the cost—is, well…tempting. Ban the guns; fewer people will be murdered, right? Ban alcohol; alcoholism will become a thing of the past. Or will it?

Sadly, it won't. Never has; never will, precisely because this world *is* fallen. Throughout history, a thriving black market has circumvented every ban imaginable. Humans will *always* find a way around prohibitions. Consider this National Archives account of the era of prohibition in the United States:

> Alcohol consumption dropped by 30 percent and the United States Brewers' Association admitted that the consumption of hard liquor was off 50 percent during Prohibition. These statistics however, do not reflect the growing disobedience toward the law and law enforcement. The intensity of the temperance advocates was matched only by the inventiveness of those who wanted to keep drinking. Enforcing Prohibition proved to be extremely difficult. The illegal production and distribution of liquor, or bootlegging, became rampant, and the national government did not have the means or desire to try to enforce every border, lake, river, and speakeasy in America. In fact, by 1925 in New York City alone there were anywhere from 30,000 to 100,000 speakeasy clubs. The demand for alcohol was outweighing (and out-winning) the demand for sobriety. People found clever ways to evade Prohibition agents. They carried hip flasks, hollowed canes, false books, and the like.[1]

This calls into question my aversion to the legalization of recreational drugs. No, I don't want marijuana or the rest of it legalized. Perhaps it is because one drug tends to lead to another and many drugs turn occasional users into addicts so rapidly. (A topic for another day, perhaps?)

And yes, I *am* in favor of banning abortion. Unlike alcohol or guns, abortion is not *potentially* harmful; it kills innocents in cold blood. Lest anyone surmise that my position is of the holier-than-thou variety, hear this loud and clear: Thirty-plus years ago, I was a proudly post-modern, independent-from-God coed, and I had an abortion. I have regretted that unspeakable act of violence with every breath since. Yet another topic for another day.

In an era of nanny states and personal dependence on impersonal government institutions, I believe more strongly than ever that personal freedoms are essential. God Himself granted us the freedom to choose or reject Him, to excel or to screw up royally, knowing full well that we would probably do our fair share of both. Our earthly parents eventually released us from our playpens into a dangerous world, knowing we could not grow unless we learned to make choices.

We cannot make choices unless we have the freedom to choose.

Tammy

"Underage drinking costs the United States more than 58 billion dollars every year—enough to buy every public school student a state-of-the-art computer."[2] While statistics like these are scary, sad, and clearly negative, I wanted to find out what the bottom-line story was. Maybe it's just the lingering effect of my school stats classes, but I have an admitted tendency to distrust statistics in general. I realize that with statements like these, someone is just trying to make a comparison that brings their point home, but I also know from experience that the numbers can be spun to say almost anything.

So I went looking for the plain and simple. I found it with the CDC (Center for Disease Control). The CDC defines "heavy drinking" as "more than two drinks per day on average for men or more than one drink per day on average for women." It also defines "binge drinking" as "five or more drinks during a single occasion for men or four or more drinks during a single occasion for women."

And the survey says: "According to recent national surveys, more than half of the adult US population drank alcohol in the past 30 days. Approximately 5 percent of the total population drank heavily, while 15 percent of the population binge drank."[3] Therefore, nearly half of the adult population had not had a drink in the past month, and of those that did, more than half qualified as "moderate" drinkers.

To me, that's about as bottom-line as it gets. Granted, that small percentage causes more than enough damage. True, about a third of traffic fatalities are "alcohol-related." But don't forget the encouraging fact that that percentage has been steadily decreasing since 1982, when it was 60 percent![4]

Honestly, I think that even as scary as the statistics often are, it's important to notice that the vast majority of the problem lies with drunkenness and underage drinking—alcohol *abuse*, which is not the same as alcohol *use*. Shae, I don't think we need another Prohibition. Like Donna pointed out, the first one didn't work anyway. I think if we enforce the laws we have—the drinking age is 21, and drunk driving is strictly illegal—we can manage the problem to the best of a fallen world's ability while maintaining those personal freedoms.

God started us off on free will, and the truth is that humans fell. Still, He didn't step in and say, "All right! That's it! You obviously can't handle yourselves, so no more freedoms for you!" If He doesn't prohibit every little thing that *can* be abused and turned to harm, then Heaven forbid I try to do it for Him!

Endnotes

1. "Teaching With Documents: The Volstead Act and Related Prohibition Documents," The National Archives, http://www.archives.gov/education/lessons/volstead-act/ (accessed August 2, 2009).

2. MADD; http://www.gdcada.org/statistics/alcohol.htm.

3. CDC; http://www.cdc.gov/alcohol.

4. http://www.alcoholalert.com/drunk-driving-statistics.html.

Your Reflections

_____

_____

_____

_____

_____

_____

_____

_____

_____

_____

_____

_____

_____

Your Reflections

_____

_____

_____

_____

_____

_____

_____

_____

_____

_____

_____

_____

_____

_____

_____

_____

_____

_____

_____

_____

_____

_____

_____

_____

_____

_____

_____

_____

_____

_____

_____

_____

Your Reflections

_____

_____

_____

_____

_____

_____

_____

_____

_____

_____

_____

_____

_____

_____

_____

PIÑA COLADAS AND THE PEARLY GATES

_____

_____

_____

_____

_____

_____

_____

_____

_____

_____

_____

_____

_____

_____

_____

_____

CHAPTER 8

Big Brother Says

Donna

The U.S. government has some tough love for imbibers. The U.S. Centers for Disease Control and Prevention says that "heavy drinking" amounts to more than two drinks per day average for men or more than one drink per day average for women.[1] (Consider this tidbit in light of the two-martini lunch.) Men who drink five or more drinks on a given occasion (four or more for women) qualify as binge drinkers.[2] How many guys and gals do that watching a football game?

There's more. "From 2001-2005, there were approximately 79,000 deaths annually attributable to excessive alcohol use. In fact, excessive alcohol use is the 3rd leading lifestyle-related cause of death for people in the United States each year."[3] (If you can't picture 79,000 people, here's a visual aid: the Stratford Stadium designed for the 2012 London Olympics will hold 80,000 people. Picture or no, that's a lot of folks.)

"You sure are piling it on," you say dryly as you pluck the olive from your stemware.

"Who me?" I ask. "I'm innocent! That's Uncle Sam speaking. Listen to what he says about American youth."

> …those who drink alcohol are more likely to be involved in homicides, suicides, and accidents; they are also at higher risk for the long-term effects of unfavorable brain development; they are more prone to abusing other drugs; they are more likely to suffer physical, memory, social, legal, school problems, and other adverse outcomes.[4]

"Thanks for the joy," you murmur as you pour another dry one to fortify your buckling knees.

"You're welcome and please don't kill the messenger," I reply. A former Surgeon General's comments in the *NIH News*[5] will make you feel even worse. But we'll let that not-so-sleeping dog lie for now. But FYI, as a driver, drinking at the legal limit is a pretty poor insurance policy against road deaths.[6]

Overall, government data list some marginal benefits of alcohol use. Perhaps it is consoling to know that a tipsy driver who perishes in a traffic accident has a lower cholesterol level than the innocent abstainer he hit head-on. However, I doubt that surviving loved ones (spouse, kids, parents, or friends) will take comfort in that silver lining. Call me crazy, prudish, parochial, boring, judgmental, puritanical, old-fashioned, narrow-minded, biased, or anything else you choose; but, for the life of me, I can't find a compelling rationale for partnering with the ol' sauce.

Tammy

In more than half of the good old U.S. of A., you can pick up your beer, wine, and other liquors at WalMart while grabbing more laundry detergent, or at the local gas station while tanking up, or even at the grocery store while picking up eggs and peanut butter. Cheers to the free market system! However, in the humble opinion of 18 out of the 50 states in our Union, alcohol constitutes a product that deserves a little extra scrutiny. The result? State governments stepping in and regulating the sale of beer, wine, and liquor, acting as the wholesaler of all alcoholic beverages to their own licensed retailers.

I happen to live in one of these "control states"—and one of the more strictly-regulated, to boot. And we Pennsylvanians sure can be funny when we visit states where alcohol is available anywhere beverages are sold. We're used to having to make a special trip to "beer and soda" or "wine and spirits" stores, where anything malt has to be bought by the case. I think we tend to forget you can pick up a six-pack at WalMart elsewhere in the country. My sister recently called me from Colorado just to tell me she saw six-packs of Mike's Hard Lemonade at the store. She was thrown for a loop…until I reminded her that it's only Pennsylvania and a few other states that make a big deal out of the ole moonshine. LOL Donna—she was actually not too far from your home sweet home at the time. ^_~

Control states choose to regulate the business like this, claiming that there are many benefits to taking a substance like alcohol out of the realm of private enterprise. For example, individual retailers—who have their profits on the line—might be tempted to sell to minors, whereas state-controlled stores have no incentive, monetary or otherwise, to allow underage customers to purchase their wares.

In addition, there are a few counties—like Montgomery County, Maryland—and a few cities that also choose to regulate the sale of alcohol. Apart from these, however, most states are "licensure states" where private sellers just need to have the right piece of paper to peddle their bubbly. In these states, the general public doesn't have to have their selection narrowed down for them by the governmental bigwigs. Supporters of the licensure model tend to pooh-pooh control states as everything from inconvenient to socialist.

Me? I have no idea. I can deal with the extra trip; on the other hand, I could live without it, too. Either way, the whole country is under one law on the drinking age—21 and not before, kiddos! Big brother says so! ^_^

Shae

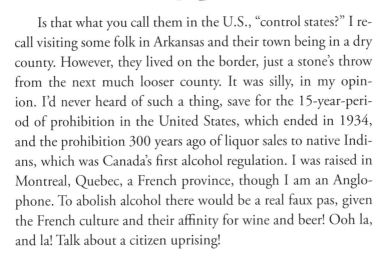

Is that what you call them in the U.S., "control states?" I recall visiting some folk in Arkansas and their town being in a dry county. However, they lived on the border, just a stone's throw from the next much looser county. It was silly, in my opinion. I'd never heard of such a thing, save for the 15-year-period of prohibition in the United States, which ended in 1934, and the prohibition 300 years ago of liquor sales to native Indians, which was Canada's first alcohol regulation. I was raised in Montreal, Quebec, a French province, though I am an Anglophone. To abolish alcohol there would be a real faux pas, given the French culture and their affinity for wine and beer! Ooh la, and la! Talk about a citizen uprising!

Canada has some of the highest rates of sin taxes in the world! A great bulk of the retail price of alcohol is federal excise tax. Provincial markups, environmental taxes, and federal and provincial sales taxes also boost the price; thus why many Canadians cross the line to the U.S. for cheaper booze (and cigarette) hauls. The sale of alcohol here contributes greatly to Canada's national economy (as does tobacco) through taxation especially, as I am sure it does in the United States. Alternatively, alcohol use and abuse contributes to a greater number of social, legal, health, and economic problems and stresses on our systems, society, and families. The cost of its abuse is in the double-digit billions. The legal drinking age is between 18 and 19 depending on the province or territory, lowered from 21 sometime in the 1970s, so you can imagine the problems we have with those youth influencing the younger 11 to 17-year-olds.

For the most part, the country has programs in place, and people are willing to get help with their struggles and addictions, especially during boom and bust periods. The government restricts the hours and days of sales, although this is loosening up considerably. Zoning laws are in place to prevent clustering of retail outlets, and the BAC limits are quite low, from 0.08 to 0.05 range.

There is a lot of illogical irony in our system, however. For instance, in 2006, the government proposed banking a complete mental health system upgrade solely with revenues gleaned from the excise tax on alcohol. But that doesn't make sense. It is like they are not expecting people to drink less, and in fact, are counting on them to drink more to pay for the initiative. But at the same time, many mental health problems are linked to alcohol addiction and abuse! Duh.

Angela

I was raised in a small town (village, really) nestled in the Cumberland Valley in southcentral Pennsylvania, and for as long as I can remember our little hamlet has been "dry." I applaud all of the town officials who over the years have chosen to keep alcohol (and drunks) off the straight and narrow public streets. No doubt the police have had their share of unruly people to tend to, but a small number compared to towns that have bars on every corner. And Tammy…I can still remember the first time I was in another state and saw alcohol on the shelves of a supermarket—BIG surprise!

As a little kid, I remember whispering with friends about the "beer and stuff" that was supposedly guzzled at the local VFW located over the hill near the community playground. As mentioned previously, my mother didn't drink, but my dear dad had a bottle of Scotch in his basement workshop that was only opened for a shot on New Year's Eve with a special friend or two. When I was a young teenager (you know, when your mind and body are taken over by aliens who make you do dumb, stupid things) for a little while there was a bottle of something hidden under the sink in the kitchen (maybe cooking sherry?) and friends and I drank enough to get sick. No wonder it was under there beside the Drano and Clorox.

Of course I'm not as naive as to think that people aren't drinking in their own home, but that's where they should be drinking. Not in a bar and then driving home and causing accidents. And, of course, I have to admit that although the drinking age in Pennsylvania has always been 21 (even during the 1960s "if I'm old enough to go to war, I should be old enough to drink a beer" mantra), I knew a lot of high schoolers who would drive to Maryland or West Virginia to get served underage. I never went on trips out of state to drink, but I did my share of pretending to like the stuff "because all the cool kids were doing it." Yeah, remember your mother saying that bit about jumping off a cliff after the cool kids…? In fact, I drank more alcohol between 19 and 21 than I ever drank after being "legal." At 25 (almost 30 years ago) I drank my last drop of alcohol, in memory of a teenager who was killed when my nephew caused an accident because he was drinking and driving. He has since stopped abusing alcohol, but the scars remain.

Endnotes

1. U.S. Department of Health and Human Services Centers for Disease Control and Prevention, "Alcohol and Public Health," http://www.cdc.gov/alcohol/ (accessed August 2, 2009).

2. Ibid.

3. Ibid.

4. U.S. Department of Health and Human Services Centers for Disease Control and Prevention, "Quick Stats: Underage Drinking," http://www.cdc.gov/alcohol/quickstats/underage_drinking.htm (accessed August 2, 2009).

5. U.S. Department of Health and Human Services, "Surgeon General Calls on Americans to Face Facts About Drinking Transportation Safety Leaders Join Alcohol Research, Prevention, and Treatment Leaders to Recommend Screenings on April 8, National Alcohol Screening Day," National Institutes of Health (NIH News), http://www.niaaa.nih.gov/NewsEvents/NewsReleases/Screenday04.htm (accessed August 2, 2009).

6. Ibid.

Your Reflections

Piña Coladas and the Pearly Gates

_____

_____

_____

_____

_____

_____

_____

_____

_____

_____

_____

_____

_____

Your Reflections

_____

_____

_____

_____

_____

_____

_____

_____

_____

_____

_____

_____

_____

_____

_____

Piña Coladas and the Pearly Gates

_____

_____

_____

_____

_____

_____

_____

_____

_____

_____

_____

_____

_____

_____

_____

CHAPTER 9

Say What?

Shae

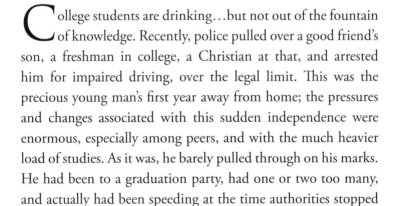

College students are drinking…but not out of the fountain of knowledge. Recently, police pulled over a good friend's son, a freshman in college, a Christian at that, and arrested him for impaired driving, over the legal limit. This was the precious young man's first year away from home; the pressures and changes associated with this sudden independence were enormous, especially among peers, and with the much heavier load of studies. As it was, he barely pulled through on his marks. He had been to a graduation party, had one or two too many, and actually had been speeding at the time authorities stopped him. Right now, he is awaiting court, and his parents have had to put out thousands of dollars in bail and legal fees, but we are all praying a good outcome because he is truly repentant, and realizes that in one fell swoop, all opportunity could go *poof.*

This episode—the mug shot, the fingerprinting, the strip search, the night in jail, the shame—scared him straight, but he is one of the fortunate ones. A new government study shows alcohol-related deaths on the rise over the last decade among college students, blaming binge drinking and drunk driving as the cause of drinking-related accidental deaths among 18- to 24-year-old students. Among all college students, the stats are clear, zero drinking after death. Jim Morrison, famed member of the musical group *The Doors,* compared drinking to gambling, "You go out for a night of drinking and you don't know where you're going to end up the next day. It could work out good or it could be disastrous. It's like the throw of a dice."

My friend's son has a great biblical foundation and upbringing upon which to rely (save for the trauma of the divorce of his parents as a youngster), but worldly influences and lures at times seem greater than the truths that he knows. On the one hand, we have the brewing companies, at least one huge one here in Canada, foisting beer as part of a healthy, normal, balanced lifestyle. This company actively engages in responsible and moderate drinking initiatives by speaking directly and positively to consumers, especially college kids, encouraging and celebrating responsible drinking. Of course, their logo is all over their educational material, and their responsible drinking messages are strewn with advertising across campuses and in gathering places. I heard that they formed a coalition of brewers to target campus networks nationwide with their responsible drinking campaigns. Is responsible drinking an oxymoron, or what? I am sure the kids are cotton to it, and enjoy the extra sideshow, free sports tickets, and favors, but ultimately, at their own expense.

Angela

Shae, the answer to your question, "Is responsible drinking an oxymoron or what?" is YES! Especially for young people who don't know which drink will lead them to a life of alcoholism, lead to killing someone in an avoidable car accident, or lead to their early death.

Our oldest daughter earned her undergraduate degree from a well-respected (Ivy League wannabe), small, private college. The beautifully landscaped campus showcases limestone buildings filled with state-of-the-art classroom technology and all the comforts college students (and their parents) expect from a school costing. (One parent likened it to "buying a new Lexus and then driving it off a cliff every year.") Founded in the late 1700s by a signer of the Declaration of Independence, an open Bible remains part of the official college seal, although the school has long since ceased to be known or even touted as a Christian college.

Freshman year was exciting for our daughter. Students from across the nation and a few other nations converged to drink from that fountain of knowledge that Shae mentioned. An accomplished French language student, our daughter chose to step out and learn German (which she dropped after a few classes of having to make too many "guttural noises"). It was a time of adventure, of trying on new ideas and interests. Mixing with others of different backgrounds and lifestyles was mind broadening and boggling.

One weekend into their second semester, a group of freshmen (all under the age of 21) got together in one of the dorm rooms (oops, I mean "residence halls") and, along with talking and getting to know each other, they were drinking. And drinking. And drinking. Shortly after midnight, one of the young men was feeling sick so he went to the window, opened it, stuck his head out to vomit, and instead fell to his death. What a tragedy. What a waste.

The student body was shaken. The faculty and staff were shocked. The parents were devastated. There was a memorial to "celebrate his life." Turns out, he was a really good guy who was on the road to a successful life, maybe filled with notable business accomplishments, a loving wife, children who adored him. During the "celebration" the undertone of sadness and sense of waste was raging. Shae's friend's son had to go through the humiliation of a strip search and a night in jail, but he has a chance to make his life right again; this young man's untimely and unnecessary death has been haunting memories for the past 19 years.

Although the student body was shaken, did they stop drinking? No…they just stayed away from open windows.

Say What?

Donna

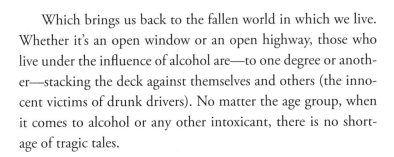

Which brings us back to the fallen world in which we live. Whether it's an open window or an open highway, those who live under the influence of alcohol are—to one degree or another—stacking the deck against themselves and others (the innocent victims of drunk drivers). No matter the age group, when it comes to alcohol or any other intoxicant, there is no shortage of tragic tales.

Whether it's in your circle or on the evening news, the dark evidence is irrefutable: lives, young and old, have been snuffed out needlessly. Countless families have been ripped apart by the excruciating trauma of alcohol-related deaths. Countless parents, their hearts rent by the loss of a child, have whispered in despair, "If only…."

High school and college youth are among the most vulnerable to alcohol. Just when they're feeling their oats and ready to fly the family coop, they find themselves on a campus with a bunch of other folks who are on the same journey—some are more secure than others and stand a better chance of survival; some are more emotionally needy and long for the attention dangerous behaviors can garner.

I remember being 17-ish, barefoot, wearing bell bottoms and "love" beads, and sitting on an old car seat in Carmine's pitch-dark basement with a bunch of friends. We'd listen to Cream or Led Zeppelin or Jimi Hendrix and say things like, "Wow, man life is deep." (Yes. We actually said things like that.)

The problem with the deep-ness of life was that we wanted to plumb those depths to their bottoms. Thankfully, some of us proceeded with caution, aware, to whatever infinitesimal degree, of life's fragility. Some plowed the depths with abandon, assured they were invincible.

All of us were searching for the answer to the same question: "Who am I, really?" Often, the answer came at a high price. One schoolmate drove his classic Chevy into a concrete overpass. Several others died in a tragic sequence of alcohol- and drug-related mishaps over the course of a single, deadly summer (or was it two?). It was a long season of sorrow in which there always seemed to be another funeral to attend.

While I'm not advocating a legalistic approach to alcohol (legalism never set anyone free), I agree with you, Angela: there's no telling which drink will prove to be the difference maker. I understand the rationale, "It's just one drink. What's the big deal?" But I also understand the law of unintended consequences. In a fallen world, collateral damage piles up fast.

At best, alcohol is a crap shoot; at worst it's Russian roulette. Some walk away nearly unscathed; some come away deeply scarred. Some never leave the scene of the accident.

Tammy

My younger brother attends a well-reputed state college—that is, it has a widespread reputation as a party school, and that's its biggest claim to fame. His school is fairly quiet on the subject of alcohol, though of course it doesn't condone law-breaking. The result? Lots of underage kids drink, and plenty of those get trashed and do stupid stuff. Still others, however, know how to have a few drinks, socialize, have fun, and stay in control of themselves.

My younger sister is a CA (paid dorm mom) at a school that, by rule, is a dry campus. The school rule is, "No drinking here, and you better be sober by the time you get back from wherever you went." Of course, that doesn't mean everyone follows the rules. My sister has had the fun experience of busting up a drinking party being held in the underclassman dorm she's in charge of—she got to call the cops and everything. On another occasion, one of the other CAs had his own drinking party in his room—and got caught, fired from his CA position, and put on probation as a student.

My other younger sister went to a private school where the common code was to study hard and party harder. The last week of school, the campus was fairly overrun by drinking parties. By contrast, my school treated alcohol as a sin and hardly anyone touched the stuff.

The college story in a nutshell is that schools all take varying stances on alcohol. However, the challenge is ubiquitous and most college students are underage, so universities have to at least make some kind of statement and plan how much effort they are going to put into enforcing their rules. All this is true because, plain and simple, most college students are irresponsible drinkers, not to mention illegal.

However, I must say I completely disagree with y'all—responsible drinking isn't an oxymoron or necessarily a contradiction. Saying that drinking responsibly cannot happen simply because more people are not responsible is like saying that saving sex for marriage cannot happen simply because most people don't. According to a 2002 study, 95 percent of Americans engaged in premarital sex. Does that make waiting impossible?[1]

I'm a proud unmarried virgin who has a few drinks on occasion, never gets drunk, and never endangers anyone by enjoying the beverages I do. I admit I'm a minority, but don't say I'm a contradiction. I'm living proof that people can drink responsibly if they choose to, and if you want to say that I just haven't had enough time to blossom into the alcoholic I'm already becoming, then look at my dad. He's 56 and drinks responsibly, too, same as I do, and he has for years.

It's possible.

Endnote

1.   http://www.publichealthreports.org/archives/issueopen.cfm?articleID=1784

Your Reflections

Piña Coladas and the Pearly Gates

_____

_____

_____

_____

_____

_____

_____

_____

_____

_____

_____

_____

_____

Your Reflections

_____

_____

_____

_____

_____

_____

_____

_____

_____

_____

_____

_____

_____

_____

_____

CHAPTER 10

Our Cuppa Whine

Donna

I t's back to square one for me. After all of our conversations on the subject of alcohol, I am pretty much where I started, or at least where I've been since shortly after coming to Christ. I'm living the dry life (and, trust me, I don't mean boring).

Call me a prude if you like. I guess for some, I qualify, having not had a drink since the 1980s. But it's not a stiff upper lip or a buttoned-down approach to life that keeps me out of the liquor store. Abstinence is not a change or a statement that I purposed to make. It's not an effort I undertook or a record I'm trying to keep. It's not emblematic of my sterling resolve or my great works. It's none of those things. Just get between me and my daily latte and you'll find that I have leanings of my own, thank you very much.

For whatever reason, I have no desire for alcohol or its use. The taste does nothing for me. Neither does the buzz. Yes, I have experienced days of celebration in which a toast might have seemed to be "the thing to do." But, when joy is in the house, it's not alcohol that makes the toast meaningful. And yes, I have experienced difficult days in which diversion seemed like an attractive alternative, days when life threw a curve ball so wide that escaping to the dugout with a drink might have seemed a logical way to ease the pain.

Which, I suppose, gets to the root of the issue for me. After all this discussion, two questions keep bobbing to the surface of my thoughts. The issue is not *whether* I drink alcohol, but *why* and *what next?* What's my motivation for drinking a substance that alters mind, emotions, and functionality? What do I want it to do for me? Is it just another beverage? And if it is, why choose it? Am I drinking it to avoid dealing with something that is causing me pain? Am I trying to drown my sorrows when they can be healed instead? Am I using alcohol to create something I lack (joy, peace, confidence, etc.)? And what happens next? Does this lead somewhere? Is it a place I really want to go?

If I could find the upside to alcohol, I would say so. But I honestly can't. Alcohol is a poison, much like tobacco is. It causes unpleasant side effects and generates negative consequences. It frankly offers me nothing of value, not when compared to the unadulterated moments in life. Whether those moments are good, bad, or ugly, I want to be 100 percent "there."

Shae

Amen, Donna, which is exactly what I have been saying all along, from my moderationist Philippians 4:5 (KJV) viewpoint. God has spoken to your heart, according to His plans and purposes for your life, according to the pattern He has for you, according to your make-up...and may have even encouraged you to abstain or deny yourself alcohol, and that's the squeeze for all of us. Moderation—with the caveat that we have to be willing to give it up without question and without hesitation. We have to be willing to deny it in the fashion of Mark 8:34, even a healthy nip if God asks. God's Word does sanction wine's use in different ways (see Deut. 14:26; Eccl. 9:7; Matt. 26:29), and does recognize some healthful aspects of alcohol (see 1 Tim. 5:23). From what I've surmised from the Bible, alcohol in moderation is seen and encouraged as a rich blessing by God, and viewed as a negative only when it is abused, as in other things. But we are living in a culture of excess. We've taken liberties and even good gifts from God to such extremes that they become our poisons. What I believe God meant to be a relaxing, nourishing effect of a glass of wine has for many become a crutch through over imbibing, and its abuse an open door for the enemy to entrap us.

The Bible actually provides case studies of others who have

arrived at personal conclusions. Take Solomon. God gave him much wisdom but he had some hard lessons to learn by experience. In fact, he describes his futile attempt to find happiness by pursing whatever physical pleasures his heart desired, the wine, women, song, partay! (See Ecclesiastes 2.) His "experiment" failed miserably, and Solomon became a candidate for suicide if ever I saw one. At the end of Ecclesiastes in chapter 12, he concludes what he learned through it all. *"...Fear God, and keep His commandments, for this is the whole duty of man. For God will bring every work into judgment."* (Ecc. 12:13-14) In other words, we will all be held accountable by our Creator for our actions. If we get drunk and do something dumb, there will be consequences one way or the other. The Bible warns us repeatedly against this behavior (see Prov. 20:1; Rom. 13:13; 1 Cor. 5:11; 6:10; Eph. 5:17-18; 1 Pet. 4:1-3).

This whole issue for Christians is one of personal responsibility as it relates to the Lord and our desire for His truth, His goodness, His beauty, and deeper relationship with Him. As such, it is not one of biblical or theological mandate or precepts, but of conformance or decisions based on personal desire for God and His nature, for obedience and the leading of the Holy Spirit to that end. The Bible says that God will reward those who walk in His ways, as well as those who overcome personal behavior problems. God Himself reveals the true purpose for human life, and He outlines *The Way* that leads to happy, healthy, fulfilling, joyful lives. When that knowledge is missing, it is almost impossible to resist the lure of the temptation to get high, or even deny ourselves of the pleasures of wine (or a closet full of shoes)! In the absence of the knowledge of the Lord and close relationship with

Him through regular prayer and devotions, I recommend abstinence. And that applies to shopping, too. @@

Angela

When our daughter and her beloved decided to have their wedding in our "family church" and the sit-down dinner reception on our home's front lawn (200+ guests!), I knew the subject of beverages would cause some angst (as in my inevitable heart attack). His big Italian-Irish family considers a beer, wine, or a good stiff drink nothing out of the ordinary. Of course, they assumed, there would be an "open bar" at the reception. I put up only a little fuss (um, well relatively speaking, depending on who you ask), as the subject seemed to be settled. I held my tongue, bit my tongue, swallowed my tongue, and finally accepted the fact that the adults who wanted to drink would be drinking—in my yard. His New York family had chartered a bus to ferry all the guests from the hotel to our "country home," which was a blessing so I didn't have to worry about impaired drivers leaving the reception. I'll never forget one of our son-in-law's groomsmen during rehearsal saying, "Wow—I've never SEEN so much corn!" as this New York City-slicker had driven by field after field of it getting to the church.

The wedding ceremony was beautiful, but the late-July weather was typical Pennsylvania hot and humid. After the procession that meandered along the Big Spring, stopping for photos on the stone one-lane bridge and under huge weeping willow trees by the fresh flowing clear water, the guests made a beeline for the refreshment station set up on one of our patios that the bride had decorated with grapevines and flowers. Always in the back of my mind was the nagging thought of something bad happening because of the presence of alcohol. As late afternoon turned into dusk and evening, a good time was had by all. By late evening, most were winding down even though the band was still blaring—no doubt the woodland wildlife is still reeling after four years. Although a few were dancing with white feather boas on their heads (part of the table centerpieces), the atmosphere was festive, not violent; joyous, not out of control; and memorable, not blacked out.

Our oldest daughter was recently married on a breath-taking beach in Florida. The family affair was a beautiful joining of lives and hearts and lots of "grand" voices. Again it was hot and humid (August in Sarasota), and there was beer and wine at the reception. But no one was unruly, no one made an unpleasant scene, no one got hurt. (Her husband is a police officer, which may have also been a contributing factor to the "good behavior.") Again, the atmosphere was one of congratulations and best wishes, hugs and joyful tears.

Would these two special events have been different if alcohol had not been served? I don't know. I'd like to think not, but in reality, the "edge" of some prickly personalities may have been smoothed away and the "baggage" of some otherwise burdened people may have been discarded...for a while.

My husband and I chose not to drink, and we had a marvelous time at both!

Tammy

LOL, Angela, I was in college before I even encountered the idea of a dry wedding. I mean, sure the university was dry, but I guess I just assumed that was because we were all underage anyway. It never occurred to me that these same folks would have the same dry ideals at a wedding. A wedding, of all things! To me, that was a mind-flip. Or a culture shock, take your pick. (To them, my surprise was out of the blue, too. Picture two people staring at each other with gaping jaws and bugging eyes— alas, a missed Kodak moment.) ^_^

Yes, I went to college and church with people who had nothing to do with alcohol and saw no purpose for it. Somehow, the paradigm they lived in just didn't rub off on me. I grew up without thinking anything of it—my dad had the occasional beer and my grandparents made wine from their own vineyard. Alcohol was around, but not ubiquitous; it was an "adult" drink, but not so taboo that I was overly interested in it; and it figured in most special occasions or celebrations, but not really in everyday life. It was just a drink—a treat for grown-ups, while I, as a kid, would get Coke on special occasions.

I realize now that the drink I'd always considered a non-issue is actually a huge sticking-point for a lot of people, but even knowing that, it's still basically the same to me. I drink it moderately. I never have too much because I never *want* that much—just not that thirsty, thanks! I reject some drinks as not to my taste, while others I find delicious.

Lastly, since I've been legal to drink, I've never felt the slightest conviction from the Holy Spirit about it. During our discussions, I've even prayed especially, asking Him if I had failed to hear His heart on this issue. I can only report that He has reassured me with His love, and that alcohol is not an issue between us.

I'm good with that. ^_^

Your Reflections

_____

_____

_____

_____

_____

_____

_____

_____

_____

_____

_____

_____

_____

_____

_____

_____

_____

_____

_____

_____

_____

_____

_____

_____

_____

_____

_____

Your Reflections

_____

_____

_____

_____

_____

_____

_____

_____

_____

_____

_____

_____

_____

_____

_____

_____

PIŃA COLADAS AND THE PEARLY GATES

_____

_____

_____

_____

_____

_____

_____

_____

_____

_____

_____

_____

_____

_____

_____

_____

CONCLUSION

The thread woven throughout our blogs seems to be that of "moderation." As Scripture, friends, statistics, and history seem to support that thread, I suppose we have come to the conclusion that as Christians who serve a God of mercy and grace, we must allow our freedom in Him to direct our choices.

As Christians we all know the "judge not as ye may be judged" 11th commandment, many times used as a way of avoiding or confronting an issue. All human beings have their weaknesses and things that pull too hard on time, effort, and interest—career, sports, beer, shoes, sex, power, wine, ice cream, fitness, *American Idol*, drugs, politics, Mt. Dew, and even ministry, just to name a few. No one is perfect, save Jesus. But God is always willing and able to help us if we've gone over to the dark side of excess.

When living in Hawaii, we attended an awesome church

with several thousand in the congregation. When they gave out bumper stickers, the pastor told people (kiddingly, with a splash of seriousness) that displaying the sticker on their car identified them as Christians and representatives of not only New Hope Christian Fellowship Oahu but also almighty God…"so don't be driving recklessly or speeding." I never put one on our car—I knew I couldn't make that no-speeding commitment.

For years, I've worn a gold cross around my neck—under my clothes. I say it's because I want to feel and be reminded of Him close to my heart. But is it really because at times I'm not a good example of what a Christian is "supposed" to be? How can we ever measure up? How can we know what may make another stumble? And as Tammy said, "What exactly do we mean by 'not causing people to stumble'? What if I'm in the company of a person who not only feels strongly that all drinking is a sin, but also has an issue of pride and looks with condemnation on others who drink? Do I cause them to stumble by quietly following my own conscience, even if they choose to judge me for it? Or do I cause them to stumble by capitulating to their conscience and allowing their prideful attitude to pass without comment? Both? Neither?"

Contrary to other religions, our God frees us from strict rules and regulations allowing us to open our hearts as He guides us in the right direction—not just regarding drinking alcohol but in every tiny or tall aspect of life. As Shae puts it, "The least can know Him in the deepest way imaginable without a smattering of theological understanding of precepts, the simplest without being bound to rules or condemned, such that a broken and rebellious teen turned wife turned divorcée turned blonde, single mother from the boonies of Canada can become an international writing evangelist, if God wills it."

Christians are free to choose. Donna's insights are right on, "In an era of nanny states and personal dependence on impersonal government institutions [in the United States], I believe more strongly than ever that personal freedoms are essential. God Himself granted us the freedom to choose or reject Him, to excel or to screw up royally, knowing full well that we would probably do our fair share of both. Our earthly parents eventually released us from our playpens into a dangerous world, knowing we could not grow unless we learned to make choices."

So raise your glass high to freedom of choice and drink fully of His love and lordship in your life!

Your Reflections

_____

_____

_____

_____

_____

_____

_____

_____

_____

_____

_____

_____

Your Reflections

_____

_____

_____

_____

_____

_____

_____

_____

_____

_____

_____

_____

_____

_____

_____

_____

_____

_____

_____

_____

_____

_____

_____

_____

_____

_____

_____

_____

_____

_____

_____

Your Reflections

_____

_____

_____

_____

_____

_____

_____

_____

_____

_____

_____

_____

_____

_____

_____

Piña Coladas and the Pearly Gates

_____

_____

_____

_____

_____

_____

_____

_____

_____

_____

_____

_____

_____

Glossary

Anglophone: English-speaker, except when facing a shoe sale.

Bigwig: A top banana, kingpin, person of influence. Alternatively, a humongous hairpiece.

BTW: By the way. But if at a Nordie's sale, Shae also uses it at times to mean, "Buy the works!"

Bubbly: Stronger than soda-pop!

Business end of a wet noodle: More "ew" than "ow" really.

Cyber-sleuthing: Mouse-driven research.

Drinking and driving: Dumb thing to do.

Dr. Kildare: Hit show of the 1960s about a dreamy young doc.

Good for what ails ya: Chocolate, sunny beaches, and the Holy Spirit. Brain-slaughtering levels of addictive substances? Not so much.

Hamlet: Small town filled with yokel locals, red necks, and assorted characters. Or ham omelet.

Haunting memories: What people have when they drink too much and do stupid things.

If you know what I mean: Used where a wink would suffice. Does anyone really know what Shae means?

IMHO: In my humble opinion.

Love beads: Hippy neckwear.

LOL: Laugh out loud.

Moonshine: Smuggled or illicitly distilled booze.

Natural high: Living your God-given destiny.

No beef: Stepping *down* from the soap-box; no argument here.

No-brainer: Opposite of rocket science.

OMG: Oh my gosh.

Ouch Chihuahua: Shaeism.

Penfolds Grange: A yummy "first growth" Australian wine of extraordinary dimension, very collectible, made predominantly from the Syrah (Shiraz) grape with a wee bit of Cabernet Sauvignon. To sip on a glass of 15-20 year old Grange is an amazing experience.

Pooh-pooh: Variation of "pfui." Snub, rebuff, repel, reject, scorn. Or, the bear of little brain, times 2.

POV: Point of view.

Rhema: (Greek) Refers to a word that is spoken, and means "utterance." The spoken word (*rhema*) of God, or revelation of the written Word (*logos*) by the Holy Spirit.

Rocky Mountain High: State of mind described in the classic John Denver tune of the same name, or an overindulgence of Rocky Road ice cream.

Smart cookies: Angela, Shae, Donna, and Tammy! Also Oreos. Yum!

St. Augustine: One cool dude who knew how to write about God.

Thrown for a loop: To confuse, shock. Picture a deer caught in headlights.

Who Moved My Cheese? Who changed these on me?

Also a terrific book by Spencer Johnson and Kenneth Blanchard.

Yowzers: Exclamation of shock and dismay, particularly at pricey shoes and booze.

^_~ Wink, wink, nudge, nudge.

:D A big, wide, (toothless?) smile!

@@ Rolling eyes skyward

ABOUT THE WRITERS

Shae Cooke is grateful that even divorce could not separate her from the love of Jesus Christ. She writes from beautiful Anmore, British Columbia, where her family and the magnificent natural wonders of her creative Father encourage her inspirational voice, heard in print worldwide. Additionally, Shae jumps into the shoes of others as a ghostwriter. A former foster child, a mother, and now in a beautiful relationship, the Lord holds copyright to her testimony, which is a work in progress. Write her at P.O. Box 78006, Port Coquitlam, B.C. Canada V3B 7H5, or visit www.Shaecooke.com.

Tammy Fitzgerald graduated from Cedarville University with a degree in English Literature, and went on to become an editor at Destiny Image Publishing Company. She also recently completed her teacher's certification at Shippensburg University. She currently lives in Pennsylvania with her cat, and has her eyes open to see where in the world God will lead her next. Contact her at tcfitzgerald1984@hotmail.com.

Donna Scuderi is a former high school English teacher and one-time rock musician who has been writing and editing professionally for more than a decade. Having served nine years in the editing department of an international ministry, she now serves a variety of individuals and organizations to perfect their message through print and public speaking. She also recently completed a feature-length screenplay. Contact Donna at readywriter77@yahoo.com.

Angela Rickabaugh Shears has been writing and editing for more than 20 years, although this trip to The Powder Room series is her first out-from-behind-the-scenes book. She earned her B.A. from the University of Hawaii–Manoa with a major in journalism/communications and a minor in political science. Visit her Web site at www.writewordsnow.com. She, her husband, Darrell, and their Old English Sheepdog Maggie, live in southcentral Pennsylvania—except when they are daydreaming about living back in Hawaii.

RECOMMENDED READING

ABC's of Emotions by Marion Meyers

After the Fall by Donald Hilliard

Dream Big by Patricia King

How to Keep Your Faith in an Upside Down World
by Sarah Bowling

Living in His Presence by Richard Booker

Release Your Anointing by T.D. Jakes

Successfully You by Leigh Valentine

Surrender to the Spirit by Keith Miller

The Love Shack by Don Nori Sr.

The Significance of One by Steve Vanzant

They Thought for Themselves by Sid Roth

What's Your Spiritual Quotient? by Mark Brewer